Practical Idea
That Really Work
for Students Who Are Gifted

Gail Ryser

Kathleen McConnell

pro·ed
An International Publisher

8700 Shoal Creek Boulevard
Austin, Texas 78757-6897
800/897-3202   Fax 800/397-7633
www.proedinc.com

© 2003 by PRO-ED, Inc.
8700 Shoal Creek Boulevard
Austin, Texas 78757-6897
800/897-3202   Fax 800/397-7633
www.proedinc.com

Printed in the United States of America

1 2 3 4 5 6 7 8 9 10   06 05 04 03 02

Contents

Introduction

We created this book, *Practical Ideas That Really Work for Students Who Are Gifted,* for educators and other school-based professionals who work with gifted students in Grades K through 12. This resource provides an assessment system and set of intervention ideas for students who are identified as gifted, have outstanding talent, or show potential for performing at high levels of accomplishment in the following areas:

- General intellectual ability
- Specific academic aptitude
- Creativity
- Leadership

The overall intent is to offer teachers a resource that is easy to use and full of practical ideas for providing differentiated instructional strategies for use with gifted students. Throughout this guide we use the term *gifted* to refer to students already identified as gifted by their local school districts, students with outstanding talents, and students who show potential for performing at high levels of accomplishment. The U.S. Department of Education used the term *talent* in its 1993 *National Excellence* report. This report was developed under the leadership of Patricia O'Connell-Ross, the director of the Javits Gifted and Talented Education Program. We believe that the ideas contained in this manual support the talent development of all students.

Components

Practical Ideas That Really Work for Students Who Are Gifted includes two components.

The Evaluation Form *with a rating scale and ideas matrix.* The rating scale portion of the Evaluation Form is a criterion-referenced measure for evaluating students' talents. Teachers rate a student on a list of behaviors, and, based on the rating, choose one or two areas to target for intervention. The ideas matrix on the last page of the Evaluation Form provides a systematic way of linking the results of the rating scale to specific interventions. We hope that educators use the matrix as a tool for selecting effective interventions to meet each student's individual needs.

A teacher-friendly Resource Manual *of practical ideas.* The ideas in this manual will assist teachers and other school-based professionals in differentiating the curriculum for gifted students. The material for each idea includes a brief explanation, followed by reproducible worksheets, examples, illustrations, and tips for easy implementation.

Development of the Rating Scale

The criterion-referenced rating scale on the Evaluation Form can be used by teachers or other school-based professionals to rate a student's talent areas. The measure was designed to assist teachers in conducting a careful and thorough assessment of specific talents in four major areas. This assessment leads to the selection of intervention strategies.

Item Development

To address the talent areas that are most relevant to educators, we consulted several sources when selecting talent areas and items for this scale. First, we examined the definition of gifted and talented children provided by the Advisory Panel to the U.S. Office of Education in 1972 in its report to Congress, *Education of the Gifted and Talented* (Marland, 1972). This definition acknowledged that students could be gifted and talented in many areas, including general intellectual ability, specific academic aptitude, creative or productive thinking, leadership ability, visual and performing arts, and psychomotor ability. The U.S. Department of Education's Office of Educational Research and Improvement (1993) issued a report, *National Excellence: A Case for Developing America's Talent,* that included a new definition. This definition also recognizes that individuals can be gifted in a number of areas and includes the following: intellectual, creative, and/or artistic areas; unusual leadership capacity; and specific academic fields. Of the five areas common to both definitions, we have included four in our rating scale. We believe that artistic talent, the fifth area, is important, but beyond the scope of this book. This book presents interventions that teachers can implement in the regular or gifted and talented classroom. Artistic talent should be recognized and encouraged, but teachers who have had training in the visual and performing arts may better serve individuals with these talents. Rating scale items for the four areas were selected after a review of the relevant literature. The resulting measure consists of 40 items; 10 items in each of the following four subscales: General Intellectual Ability, Specific Academic Aptitude, Creativity, and Leadership.

Responses to the items in the scale are based on a 5-point Likert system, with a 0 meaning *never or rarely exhibits the behavior in comparison to age peers* and a 4 meaning *exhibits the behavior much more in comparison to age peers*. After rating the items, the educator should total the scores, and begin developing differentiated instructional strategies in the area receiving the highest score. If more than one area receives high scores (i.e., >35), the teacher should develop differentiated instructional strategies in all areas receiving high scores.

Field-Testing the Rating Scale

The criterion-referenced rating scale was field-tested in several school districts in Texas with 72 students. Thirty-eight of these students were identified as gifted by their local school districts, whereas the other 34 students were not identified. Thirty-five students were male (20 identified as gifted, 15 not identified) and 37 students were female (18 identified as gifted, 19 not identified). Forty-one students were European American (21 identified as gifted, 20 not identified); 7 were African American (3 identified as gifted, 4 not identified); 13 were Hispanic American (6 identified as gifted, 7 not identified); and 11 were Asian American (8 identified as gifted, 3 not identified). All students were in Grades 1 through 11.

We conducted an item analysis using the sample of students identified as gifted. The resulting reliability coefficients were .95 for the General Intellectual Ability subscale, .96 for the Specific Academic Aptitude subscale, .94 for the Creativity subscale, and .92 for the Leadership subscale. The magnitude of these coefficients strongly suggests that the rating scale possesses little test error and that users can have confidence in its results.

In addition, we compared the mean ratings of the four subscales for the two groups, students identified as gifted and students not identified, using a *t* ratio. Our hypothesis was that students identified as gifted would be rated higher than students not identified as gifted. Because we made four comparisons for each group, we used the Bonferroni method (Feller, 1968) to adjust the alpha level and set alpha at .01. In each case the mean differences between the two groups were large enough to support our hypothesis. The probability in all cases was <.001. We can conclude that the rating scale is sensitive enough to discriminate between students identified as gifted and students not identified.

Development of the Manual

Teachers and other school-based personnel have many responsibilities and duties as part of their role in schools. In our discussions with teachers, supervisors, and counselors about the development of this product, they consistently emphasized the need for materials that are practical, easy to implement in the classroom, and not overly time consuming. We appreciate their input and worked hard to meet their criteria as we developed the ideas in this book. In addition, we conducted an extensive review of the literature, so that we would present only those ideas that were supported by data documenting their effectiveness. The result is a book with 30 ideas, nearly all with reproducible masters, and all grounded in the research and the collective experience of the two coauthors, as well as the many educators who advised us and shared information with us.

Assessment often provides much useful information to educators about the strengths of students. However, unless the information gathered during the assessment process affects instruction, its usefulness for school-based staff is limited. With this in mind, we designed an ideas matrix (see Evaluation Form) so that educators can directly link the data generated by the rating scale to instruction. This format allows us to provide information that is practical and useful.

Directions for Using the Materials

Step 1: Collect Student Information

The first step for using these materials is to complete the first page of information on the Evaluation Form for a student who is identified as gifted or who is in need of differentiated curriculum because of talents or potential talent he or she may have in the four areas covered by the scale. As an example, Rodney's completed Evaluation Form is provided in Figure 1. Space is provided on the front of the form for pertinent information about the student being rated, including name, birth date, age, school, grade, rater, and educational setting. In addition, the dates the student is observed and the amount of time the rater spends with the student can be recorded here. Also included on the front of the form is space to record the student's talent areas and the instructional strategies that have been implemented previously.

Step 2: Rate the Behaviors of the Student

Pages 2 and 3 of the Evaluation Form contain the rating scale. The items are divided into the four areas discussed previously. Instructions for administering and scoring the items are provided on the form.

Step 3: Generate an Intervention Plan

Page 4 of the Evaluation Form contains the ideas matrix, which should be consulted to determine differentiated instructional strategies to support a student's talents. After choosing the area(s) to target for differentiation (i.e., the area(s) with the highest scores), the rater turns to the ideas matrix and selects instructional strategies that relate to the target talent area. The teacher previews the selected strategies and chooses one to three ideas to implement.

For example, Rodney received the highest ratings in the area of Creativity. His teacher has targeted the area and chose Ideas 1, 6, and 21 from the ideas matrix.

Step 4: Read and Review the Practical Ideas That Have Been Selected

The teacher should read the explanation and other materials in this manual for each idea selected in Step 3. To aid in implementation, nearly all of the ideas have at least one reproducible form immediately following the explanation. Ideally, the teacher or other professional should also decide how and when to evaluate the effectiveness of each strategy selected. In our example with Rodney, this could be accomplished through self-evaluation, product development, or portfolio assessment.

Step 5: Implement the Idea

After the teacher is familiar with the idea and has prepared all necessary materials, implementation can begin. The ideas selected for implementation can easily be integrated into an overall instructional design that reflects good instructional practices for gifted students.

References

Feller, W. (1968). *An introduction to probability theory and its applications* (Vol. 1, 3rd ed.). New York: Wiley.

Marland, S. P. (1972). *Education of the gifted and talented. Report to the Congress of the United States* (2 vols.). Washington, DC: U.S. Government Printing Office.

U.S. Department of Education, Office of Educational Research and Improvement. (1993). *National excellence: A case for developing America's talent.* Washington, DC: U.S. Government Printing Office.

Research Supporting the Practical Ideas

This section provides references that have supporting data for the practical ideas in this book. These references will give relevant information to interested professionals who want to learn more about the interventions we have described. The references are grouped by general category, according to our focus during our research.

Teaching Critical and Creative Thinking Skills

Cramond, B. (2001). Fostering creative thinking. In F. A. Karnes & S. M. Bean (Eds.), *Methods and materials for teaching the gifted.* Waco, TX: Prufrock Press.

Csikszentmihalyi, M. (1996). *Creativity.* New York: HarperCollins.

Piirto, J. (1998). *Understanding those who create.* Scottsdale, AZ: Gifted Psychology Press.

Torrance, E. P., & Goff, K. (1989). A quiet revolution. *Journal of Creative Behavior, 23*(2), 136–145.

Implementing Independent Study

Betts, G. T., & Kercher, J. K. (1999). *The autonomous learner model: Optimizing ability.* Greeley, CO: Autonomous Learning Publications Specialists.

Bishop, K. (2000). The research processes of gifted students: A case study. *Gifted Child Quarterly, 44*(1), 54–64.

Johnsen, S. (2001). Teaching gifted students through independent study. In F. A. Karnes & S. M. Bean (Eds.), *Methods and materials for teaching the gifted.* Waco, TX: Prufrock Press.

Using Effective Questioning Strategies

Dantonio, M., & Beisenherz, P. C. (2001). *Learning to question, questioning to learn: A guide to developing effective teacher questioning practices.* Needham Heights, MA: Allyn & Bacon.

Paul, R. (1990). *Critical thinking: What every person needs to survive in a rapidly changing world.* Rohnert Park, CA: Center for Critical Thinking and Moral Critique.

Johnsen, S., & Ryser, G. R. (1996). An overview of effective practices with gifted students in general-education settings. *Journal for the Education of the Gifted, 19*(4), 379–404.

Structuring Group Learning

Fuchs, L. S., Fuchs, D., Hamlett, C. L., & Karns, K. (1998). High-achieving students' interactions and performance on complex mathematical tasks as a function of homogeneous and heterogeneous pairings. *American Educational Research Journal, 35*(2), 227–267.

Kenny, D. A., Archambault, F. X., Jr., & Hallmark, B. W. (1995). *The effects of group composition on gifted and non-gifted elementary students in cooperative learning groups* (Research Monograph 95116). Storrs: National Research Center on the Gifted and Talented, University of Connecticut.

Rogers, K. B. (1993). Grouping the gifted and talented: Questions and answers. *Roeper Review, 16*(1), 8–12.

Teaching Problem-Solving Skills

Reid, C., Udall, A., Romanoff, B., & Algozzine, B. (1999). Comparison of traditional and problem-solving assessment criteria. *Gifted Child Quarterly, 43*(4), 252–264.

Schack, G. D. (1993). Effects of a creative problem-solving curriculum on students of varying ability levels. *Gifted Child Quarterly, 37*(1), 32–38.

Stepien, W. J., & Gallagher, S. A. (1993). Problem based learning: As authentic as it gets. *Educational Leadership, 50*(7), 25–28.

Developing Leadership

Karnes, F. A., & Bean, S. M. (1995). *Leadership for students: A practical guide for ages 8–18.* Waco, TX: Prufrock Press.

Reilly, J. (1992). *Mentorship: The essential guide for schools and business.* Dayton: Ohio Psychology Press.

Roach, A. A., Wyman, L. T., Brookes, H., Chaves, C., Heath, S. B., & Valdes, G. (1999). Leadership giftedness: Models revisited. *Gifted Child Quarterly, 43*(1), 13–24.

Enriching and Accelerating the Curriculum

Assouline, S., Colangelo, N., Lupkowski-Shoplik, A., & Lipscomb, J. (1998). *Iowa acceleration scale: A guide to whole-grade acceleration K–8.* Scottsdale, AZ: Gifted Psychology Press.

Colangelo, N., & Davis, G. A. (1997). *Handbook of gifted education* (2nd ed.). Needham Heights, MA: Allyn & Bacon.

Reis, S. M., & Renzulli, J. S. (1992). Using curriculum compacting to challenge the above-average. *Educational Leadership, 50*(2), 51–57.

Van Tassel-Baska, J. (1992). *Planning effective curriculum for gifted learners.* Denver, CO: Love.

Practical Ideas
That Really Work
for Students Who Are Gifted

Gail Ryser
Kathleen McConnell

Evaluation Form

Name ___Rodney S.___

Birth Date ___16-15-91___   Age ___12___

School ___Jefferson Middle School___   Grade ___7___

Rater ___Ms. Murphy___

Educational Setting ___English___

Dates Student Observed: From ___9-25___ To ___11-3___

Amount of Time Spent with Student:

Per Day ___1 hour___   Per Week ___5 hours___

Student's Talent Areas

1. ___creative writing___
2. ___foreign language___
3. ___English___
4. _____

Instructional Strategies Previously Implemented

1. ___independent study___
2. ___acceleration in English___
3. _____
4. _____

A Definition of Children with Exceptional Talent

Children and youth with outstanding talent perform or show the potential for performing at remarkably high levels of accomplishment when compared with others of their age, experience, or environment.

These children and youth exhibit high performance capability in intellectual, creative, and/or artistic areas; possess an unusual leadership capacity; or excel in specific academic fields. They require services or activities not ordinarily provided by the schools.

Outstanding talents are present in children and youth from all cultural groups, across all economic strata, and in all areas of human endeavor.

Note. From *National Excellence: A Case for Developing America's Talent*, 1993, Washington, DC: U.S. Department of Education, Office of Educational Research and Improvement.

Figure 1. Sample Evaluation Form, filled out for Rodney.

Rating Scale

DIRECTIONS

❶ Read each statement and decide how often the student you are rating exhibits each behavior. As you respond, ask yourself, "To what degree does the student exhibit the behavior when compared with his or her age peers?" Use the following scale to circle the appropriate number:

0 = Never or rarely exhibits the behavior in comparison to age peers

1 = Infrequently exhibits the behavior in comparison to age peers

2 = Exhibits the behavior about the same amount as age peers

3 = Exhibits the behavior somewhat more than age peers

4 = Exhibits the behavior much more than age peers

❷ Write the total for each talent area in the box provided.

❸ Check the talent area(s) with the highest total.

❹ For each area checked, select up to three ideas from the Ideas Matrix on page 4. Write the idea number and start date for each idea in the blanks provided in the last column.

BEHAVIOR	RATING (Compared to age peers)	TOTAL	HIGHEST SCORE	IDEA NUMBER; START DATE

General Intellectual Ability

Rating scale columns: Never / Infrequently / Same / Somewhat More / Much More

1 Asks many "why" questions — 0 1 2 ③ 4

2 Is willing to revise conclusions based on new evidence — 0 1 2 ③ 4

3 Effectively synthesizes newly acquired information — 0 1 2 ③ 4

4 Is insightful — 0 1 2 3 ④

5 Searches for many solutions to a problem — 0 1 ② 3 4

6 Desires to understand how things work at a deep level — 0 1 2 ③ 4

Total: 33

7 Learns new information quickly — 0 1 2 3 ④

8 Reasons critically — 0 1 2 3 ④

9 Enjoys challenges — 0 1 2 ③ 4

10 Is an alert and keen observer — 0 1 2 3 ④

Specific Academic Aptitude (These items relate to the student's academic talent area.)

1 Possesses a large amount of information — 0 1 2 ③ 4

2 Shows an advanced level of knowledge — 0 1 2 ③ 4

3 Seeks out and reads nonfiction books — 0 1 ② 3 4

4 Has passion for academic subject area — 0 1 2 3 ④

5 Researches topics of interest — 0 1 ② 3 4

6 Is persistent when engaged in investigations — 0 1 ② 3 4

Total: 30

7 Understands advanced-level concepts — 0 1 2 ③ 4

8 Offers original interpretations to questions and issues — 0 1 2 3 ④

9 Self-motivated to do excellent work — 0 1 2 3 ④

10 Asks complex questions — 0 1 2 ③ 4

2

Figure 1. Continued.

BEHAVIOR	RATING (Compared to age peers)					TOTAL	HIGHEST SCORE	IDEA NUMBER; START DATE
	Never	Infrequently	Same	Somewhat More	Much More			

Creativity

1	Elaborates and embellishes stories or drawings	0	1	2	3	(4)			
2	Is flexible when developing ideas or solutions	0	1	2	(3)	4			
3	Is open to new experiences	0	1	2	3	(4)			
4	Is unconcerned with impressing others; individualistic	0	1	2	3	(4)			6 11-4
5	Is passionate about own creative work	0	1	2	3	(4)	38	✓	1 11-15
6	Is persistent in developing products	0	1	2	3	(4)			21 12-3
7	Has tolerance for ambiguity	0	1	2	(3)	4			
8	Demonstrates a richness of imagery in language	0	1	2	3	(4)			
9	Makes unusual connections between ideas or thoughts	0	1	2	3	(4)			
10	Produces imaginative products even if defective in quality	0	1	2	3	(4)			

Leadership

1	Is involved in the community	0	1	(2)	3	4			
2	Can effectively communicate ideas to a variety of audiences	0	1	2	(3)	4			
3	Participates in extracurricular activities	0	1	(2)	3	4			
4	Is able to motivate others	0	1	(2)	3	4			
5	Shows sensitivity to others	0	1	2	(3)	4	25	○	
6	Shows an unusual interest in societal problems	0	1	(2)	3	4			
7	Is understanding and sympathetic	0	1	(2)	3	4			
8	Sets goals and desires to achieve them	0	1	2	(3)	4			
9	Sets high standards for self	0	1	2	3	(4)			
10	Is sought out and looked up to by peers	0	1	(2)	3	4			

3

Figure 1. Continued.

Ideas Matrix

Ideas	GENERAL INTELLECTUAL ABILITY	SPECIFIC ACADEMIC APTITUDE	CREATIVITY	LEADERSHIP
1 Solve a Mess with CPS	X	X	X	X
2 Use Independent Study	X	X	X	X
3 Get Different	X	X	X	
4 Critical and Creative Thinking Skills	X		X	
5 Learning in Centers	X	X	X	X
6 Design a WebQuest	X	X	X	
7 Diagnostic–Prescriptive Method		X		
8 Contracting		X		
9 Accelerate	X	X		
10 Questions and Answers		X	X	
11 Beat the Pro	X	X		
12 Easy as Pie, Tough as Nails	X	X	X	
13 Socratic Starters	X	X		
14 Socratic Discussion	X	X		
15 Outline Line	X	X		
16 Three A's and a C		X		
17 Create Jigsaw Groups	X	X		
18 Backwards Brainstorming	X	X	X	
19 Develop a Rubric		X		
20 Create a Choice Sheet		X		
21 Keep a Portfolio		X	X	
22 One-Minute Quiz		X		
23 I Don't Get It		X		
24 MoD Squad				X
25 Listen To Lead				X
26 Three Ways To Think About Leaders				X
27 Promote Service Learning		X		X
28 Pair Students with a Mentor	X	X		X
29 SMART Goals/FINE Decisions				X
30 What Can Parents and Teachers Do To Foster Talent?	X	X	X	X

4

Figure 1. Continued.

Idea 1

Solve a Mess with CPS
(Creative Problem Solving)

Alex Osborn and Sidney Parnes formulated and researched Creative Problem Solving (CPS). Alex Osborn, creator of brainstorming, was the founder of the Creative Education Foundation and cofounder of a highly successful New York advertising agency. Sidney Parnes, followed Osborn as president of the Creative Education Foundation. CPS is versatile and helpful in identifying novel and useful solutions to problems. CPS works best when engaged in real-life problems and situations. For example, students could use it to solve school or personal issues. You also may use it at the beginning of a thematic unit to get your students thinking ahead or use it at the end as a tool to synthesize what has been learned. Some problems can be completed in 1 or 2 hours, others may take a week or more.

CPS consists of the six steps listed below (or sometimes five if there is a predefined mess to study).

❶ Mess-Finding

❷ Fact-Finding

❸ Problem-Finding

❹ Idea-Finding

❺ Solution-Finding

❻ Acceptance-Finding

Here's how it works.

❶ **Mess-Finding**

Students using CPS usually define the mess as the first step in the process, but at times the teacher may want to predefine the mess. Identify the mess by asking who, what, when, where, why.

Students should consider these issues when defining the mess:

✓ Can I do something about this? Can I take action? Do I have the resources?

☞ **Tip:**

Using the reproducible forms for Idea 1, laminate the steps and cut out and laminate one of the footprints. Use the footprint to track the CPS process by clipping the footprint with a clothespin or paperclip in front of the step on which you are currently working.

✓ Is this something that I really care about?

✓ Do I need to develop new alternatives than those that already exist for dealing with this?

The mess should be a rough statement of the problem or situation. For example, if your mess involves your school, several plausible messes might focus on the following:

* school grounds have a lot of litter,

* school could be safer for students and teachers,

* classrooms are unattractive,

* parent and community involvement is poor, or

* relationship and respect level between students and faculty needs improvement.

❷ Fact-Finding

The outcome of this step is to end up with a good description of the current situation. The students' task is to clarify the problem by collecting information. To do this, students should brainstorm and gather questions, data, or feelings that are involved in the mess. It is important not to stop this step prematurely. One method to use to help students gather facts is to compare the desired future state with the current situation to delineate the desired outcome, the opportunities that exist to get you there, and the obstacles that keep you from attaining it.

❸ Problem-Finding

This is one of the most important steps in the CPS process. The goal is to develop a clearly defined, focused, and useful problem statement. Questioning strategies are very helpful during this step. Some of the questioning strategies you might use are presented in Idea 13, Socratic Starters. In addition, IWWMW is a questioning strategy used frequently during this stage. IWWMW stands for "In what ways might we…?" Using this sentence stem forces one to state the problem in a positive rather than negative orientation. We have included a reproducible form students can use to generate problems using IWWMW.

❹ Idea-Finding

This is the stage during which students develop a list of potential solutions to the problem statement that seem promising. Every effort should be made to be as divergent as possible. Brainstorming is a good technique to use during the first phase of this step.

The critical elements of brainstorming are as follows:

❖ Don't criticize

❖ Try to think of wild or different ideas

- ❖ Generate as many ideas as possible (quantity is important here)
- ❖ Feel free to combine your idea with someone else's to make another idea

After brainstorming, students need to be convergent to create a list of the ideas that have potential. To be effective at convergent thinking, have students do the following:

- ✳ Consider both positives and negatives of each idea
- ✳ Determine if an idea is both creative and useful
- ✳ Be methodical and examine every idea before discarding or keeping it and moving on

❺ **Solution-Finding**

The outcome of this step is to select the idea with the most potential for solving the problem. During this step, students will evaluate the ideas with the greatest potential to determine which idea is the best solution. See Idea 4, Critical and Creative Thinking Skills, for a method for making and using an evaluation grid. Criteria to consider might include cost, resources, acceptance, time, and effort.

❻ **Acceptance-Finding**

The outcome of this step is to write a plan and work out the details. During this step, students will problem-solve about the issues of acceptance and implementation. Students will want to identify possible assisters and resistors, which are not only people but also anything that will increase or decrease the chances of successfully implementing the plan. It is important to identify resistors so that students can try to avoid or prevent them from occurring or at least consider ways to overcome them if they do occur. We have included two reproducible forms (one for younger students and one for older students) to use to write the action plan.

Creative Problem Solving

Step 1: Mess-Finding

Step 2: Fact-Finding

Step 3: Problem-Finding

Step 4: Idea-Finding

Step 5: Solution-Finding

Step 6: Acceptance-Finding

Idea 1

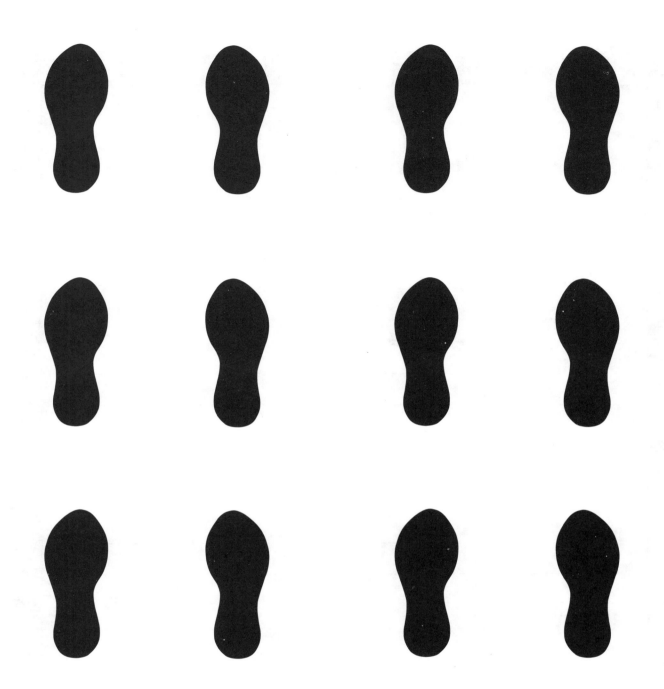

13

IWWMW
In what ways might we ...?

IWWMW_____

_____ ?

IWWMW_____

_____ ?

IWWMW_____

_____ ?

IWWMW_____

_____ ?

IWWMW_____

_____ ?

IWWMW_____

_____ ?

IWWMW_____

_____ ?

Idea 1

Action Plan

Solution _____

What?	Who Will Help?	When?
1. _____	_____	_____
2. _____	_____	_____
3. _____	_____	_____
4. _____	_____	_____
5. _____	_____	_____

Action Plan

Solution _____

	Objective	People Responsible	Timeline	Evaluation
1.				
2.				
3.				
4.				
5.				
6.				
7.				
8.				
9.				
10.				

Idea 2

Use Independent Study

Independent study is one of the most widely used strategies to adapt instruction for gifted students. Too often, teachers assume that because a student is gifted, he or she has the skills necessary for conducting an independent study project. All students need guidance, and an independent study is a planned research process. Teachers need to be actively involved in the process, at least in the beginning, and understand the guidelines to follow when assisting their students.

Here are the steps to follow.

❶ **Select a topic.**

Students must first select something they want to study. This can be a problem to solve, something to learn how to do, a hypothesis to investigate, an issue to resolve, or something to learn more about. When selecting a topic students should focus on what interests them and what topic has the most available information. Students having difficulty selecting a topic can complete the Interest Survey form as a starting point.

❷ **Maintain a schedule.**

Students can use the Timeline form to set due dates for each step and the Action Plan form to record the completion of each step. This will help students maintain a schedule and stick to it.

Self-Evaluation

Circle the letter that answers how well you completed each statement.

	EXCELLENT	OKAY	POOR
1. I selected a topic that was interesting to me.	E	O	P
2. I asked open-ended questions about my topic.	E	O	P
3. The study method I used was helpful for learning about my topic.	E	O	P
4. I worked well independently.	E	O	P
5. I completed each step on time.	E	O	P
6. My product was creative.	E	O	P
7. I presented my product to an audience who was interested in my results.	E	O	P
8. My presentation was well organized.	E	O	P
9. I should receive the following grade on my independent study project:	A	B	C

10. What will I do differently in my next independent study? _I will use my photography skills in developing my product._

❸ Ask questions.

Teachers should help students develop good questions. Good questions are generally open-ended. Some students will need a minilesson describing the difference between closed and open questions. Closed questions require identifying recall and right/wrong answers, whereas open questions require complex and divergent answers. Another strategy is to teach students to ask questions with W+H stems (i.e., who, what, when, where, why, how) and to change W+H stem questions to higher level questions (see Idea 12, Easy as Pie, Tough as Nails). Finally, students can use the SCAMPER form to generate additional questions if they get stuck (Eberle, 1984).

❹ Choose a method to research the topic.

Often students think that the only way to conduct research is to use books or the Internet to look up information and then write a report. There are actually many study methods. Some of these methods include examine historical information; conduct an experiment; record oral histories about a person's life; survey people about an idea; and make observations of people, places, and events. Teachers will want provide guidance to students in the study method they choose.

❺ Develop a product to share.

There are many products students can develop to share their results. We have included a number of these on the Product Possibilities form (also see Idea 3, Get Different, for more products). In addition to thinking about what type of product to develop, students will want to choose an appropriate audience with whom to share the results. For example, a student may share the results of a school-wide survey on safety with the principal and other campus administrators and teachers. Or a student may share an oral history of the oldest citizen in town with members of the chamber of commerce. Or a student may share an experiment investigating the effects of physical and chemical changes in the environment with the science class.

❻ Evaluate the study.

An important final step in the process is conducting a self-evaluation. This may go hand in hand with an evaluation from the teacher or facilitator, but as students become more adept, they may only do a self-evaluation with input from the teacher or facilitator. Students can use the Self-Evaluation form we have provided.

Reference. Eberle, B. (1984). *SCAMPER on.* Buffalo, NY: DOK.

Note. The Product Possibilities form is adapted from *The Ultimate Guide for Student Product Development and Evaluation* (p. 2), by F. A. Karnes and K. R. Stephens, 2000, Waco, TX: Prufrock Press. Copyright 2000 by Prufrock Press. Adapted with permission.

Interest Survey

1. What are your favorite types of books to read?
   _____

2. What hobbies do you have?
   _____

3. How do you like to spend your spare time?
   _____

4. If you could design a new class for your school, what would you design?
   _____

5. If you were going to write a story, what would you write about?
   _____

6. What countries would you like to visit?
   _____

7. Suppose you found a time machine. What time period would you travel to?
   _____

8. Do you enjoy

◆ Drawing, painting, sketching	❏ yes	❏ no
◆ Building, making constructions	❏ yes	❏ no
◆ Putting on plays, singing, acting	❏ yes	❏ no
◆ Traveling, hiking, exploring	❏ yes	❏ no
◆ Cooking, gardening	❏ yes	❏ no
◆ Playing sports, being active	❏ yes	❏ no
◆ Dancing, moving	❏ yes	❏ no
◆ Caring for animals, people	❏ yes	❏ no
◆ Collecting, experimenting	❏ yes	❏ no

☞ Now read through your answers and either alone or with your teacher, brainstorm two or three topics you would like to study.

_____

_____

_____

Timeline

Step	Due Date
Selection of Topic	_____
Develop Questions	_____
Choose Study Method	_____
Conduct Research	_____
Develop Product	_____
Present Final Results	_____

Timeline

Step	Due Date
Selection of Topic	_____
Develop Questions	_____
Choose Study Method	_____
Conduct Research	_____
Develop Product	_____
Present Final Results	_____

Idea 2

Action Plan

▼ I will study this topic:

_____

▼ Major questions:

_____

_____

_____

▼ Minor questions:

_____

_____

_____

▼ I will use this study method:

_____

▼ I will develop this product:

_____

▼ I will share my product with the following audience:

_____

Idea 2

SCAMPER

To help you ask good questions, use the technique called SCAMPER. SCAMPER stands for

S Substitute
C Combine
A Adjust
M Modify: Magnify or Minify
P Put to Other Uses
E Eliminate
R Reverse or Rearrange

✎ **Write two or more open-ended questions.** ✎

_____

_____

➤ **S**ubstitute one or more words in your questions to make them different.

_____

➤ **C**ombine two or more of your questions.

_____

➤ **A**djust your questions to make them focus on something different.

_____

➤ **M**odify your questions by making them broader (magnify) or more focused or narrow (minify).

_____

➤ **P**ut parts of your questions to different uses so they can be used to find out different things.

_____

_____

➤ **E**liminate redundant questions or some of the words in your questions.

_____

_____

➤ **R**earrange or reverse the words in your questions.

_____

Idea 2

Product Possibilities

Abstract	Cookbook	Graph
Acronym	Cooked Concoction	Graphic
Activity Sheet	Costume	Graphic Organizer
Advertisement	Crest	Greeting Card
Alphabet Book	Cross Section	Guest Speaker
Animation	Crossword Puzzle	Guide
Annotated Bibliography	Dance	Handbook
Aquarium	Database	Hidden Picture
Archive	Debate	Histogram
Art Gallery	Demonstration	Hologram
Autobiography	Design	How-to Book
Banner	Diagram	Hypermedia
Bibliography	Dialogue	Hypothesis
Biography	Diary	Illusion
Blueprint	Dictionary	Illustrated Story
Board Game	Diorama	Illustration
Book	Display	Index Cards
Book Jacket	Document	Instructions
Bookmark	Documentary	Internet Search
Book Review	Doll	Interview
Broadcast	Dramatization	Invention
Brochure	Drawing	Investigation
Budget	Editorial	Itinerary
Bulletin Board	Equation	Jewelry
Bumper Sticker	Essay	Jigsaw Puzzle
Business Plan	Etching	Jingle
Button	Evaluation Checklist	Journal
Campaign	Event	Kit
Cartoon	Exhibit	Laser Show
Carving	Experiment	Law
Catalog	Fact File	Learning Center
Celebration	Fairy Tale	Lecture
Chart	Family Tree	Lesson
Club	Field Experience	Letter
Coat of Arms	Film	Limerick
Collage	Flag	List
Collection	Flannel Board	Literary Analysis
Coloring Book	Flip Book	Log
Comedy Skit	Flowchart	Logic Puzzle
Comic Strip	Flyer	Logo
Commentary	Folder Game	Machine
Commercial	Fractal	Magazine
Competition	Game	Magazine Article
Computer Document	Game Show	Magic Show
Computer Program	Geodesics	Manual
Conference	Geometric	Manuscript
Construction	Glossary	Map with Key

Mask	Pie Chart	Sign
Matrix	Plan	Silk Screening
Menu	Plaque	Simulation
Metaphor	Play	Sketch
Mini-Center	Poem	Skit
Mobile	Pointillism	Slide Show
Mock Trial	Political Cartoon	Sociogram
Model	Pop-Up Book	Song
Monologue	Portfolio	Speech
Montage	Portrait	Spreadsheet
Monument	Position Paper	Stage Setting
Mosaic	Poster	Stained Glass
Motto	Prediction	Stamp
Multimedia Presentation	Presentation	Stencil
Mural	Program	Stitchery
Museum	Project Cube	Story
Musical Composition	Prototype	Storyboard
Musical Instrument	Puppet	Summary
Musical Performance	Puppet Show	Survey
Mystery	Questionnaire	Table
Narrative	Quilt	Tape Recording
Needlecraft	Quotations	Television Show
Newsletter	Radio Show	Terrarium
Newspaper	Rap	Tessellation
Novel	Rebus Story	Test
Oral Report	Recipe	Textbook
Organization	Recitation	Theory
Origami	Relief Map	Three-D (3-D) Model
Ornament	Report	Time Capsule
Outline	Riddle	Timeline
Overhead Transparency	Role Play	Toy
Packet	Routine	Trademark
Painting	Rubber Stamp	Travelogue
Pamphlet	Rubbing	Triptych
Panel Discussion	Rubric	Venn Diagram
Pantomime	Samples	Video
Papier-Mâché	Sand Casting	Video Game
Pattern	Scavenger Hunt	Virtual Field Trip
Performance	Scenario	Vocabulary List
Personal Experience	Science Fiction Story	Wall Hanging
Petition	Scrapbook	Watercolor
Photo Album	Script	Weaving
Photo Essay	Sculpture	Webbing
Photograph	Self-Portrait	Web Page
Photojournalism	Seminar	Woodworking
Pictograph	Service Project	Word Puzzle
Pictorial Essay	Shadow Box	Written Paper
Picture Dictionary	Shadow Play	
Picture Story	Short Story	

Idea 2

Self-Evaluation

Circle the letter that answers how well you completed each statement.

	EXCELLENT	OKAY	POOR
1. I selected a topic that was interesting to me.	E	O	P
2. I asked open-ended questions about my topic.	E	O	P
3. The study method I used was helpful for learning about my topic.	E	O	P
4. I worked well independently.	E	O	P
5. I completed each step on time.	E	O	P
6. My product was creative.	E	O	P
7. I presented my product to an audience who was interested in my results.	E	O	P
8. My presentation was well organized.	E	O	P
9. I should receive the following grade on my independent study project:	A	B	C

10. What will I do differently in my next independent study? _____

_____

Idea 2

Self-Evaluation

Circle the face that best describes how you feel about each statement.

1. I chose a topic I liked. ☺ ☹

2. I asked good questions. ☺ ☹

3. I knew how to use my study method. ☺ ☹

4. I worked well independently. ☺ ☹

5. I finished on time. ☺ ☹

6. My product was creative. ☺ ☹

7. My audience liked my presentation. ☺ ☹

Idea 2

Idea 3

Get Different

When teaching gifted students, we often seek to provide them with opportunities to demonstrate learning that results in product development and production. Product production often encourages students to demonstrate unique, divergent thinking, either individually or as a member of a group. Here is an easy way to ensure that students create a variety of visible products, rather than sticking with familiar, commonly used formats.

We have provided several sets of Get Different cards. The cards can be used in making random assignments of products to students. Just shuffle each deck and allow individual students or student groups to pick a card. That way, you make sure that students demonstrate and share their knowledge in many different ways. They learn not just content but several styles of data presentation and a variety of formats in which they can present information.

Make a

Display

Make a

Fact File

Create an

Experiment

Design a

Game

Design a

Computer Program

Make a

Model

Make a

Project Cube

Make a

Detailed Illustration

Design a

Web Page

Create a

Map

Idea 3

Make a
Chart

Create a
Diagram with Labels

Language Arts/Social Studies

Create an
Advertisement

Write a
Rebus Story

Create a
Flip Book

Write a
Newspaper Story

Design a
Puppet

Create a
Picture Story

Write a
TV/Radio Script

Create a
Photo Essay

Idea 3

Write a
Poem

Create a
Diorama

Create an
Oral Report

Write a
Fairy Tale

Design a
Mural

Create a
Family Tree

Create a
Map with Legend

Create a
Comic Strip

All Content Areas

Create a
Pamphlet

Write an
Editorial

Idea 3

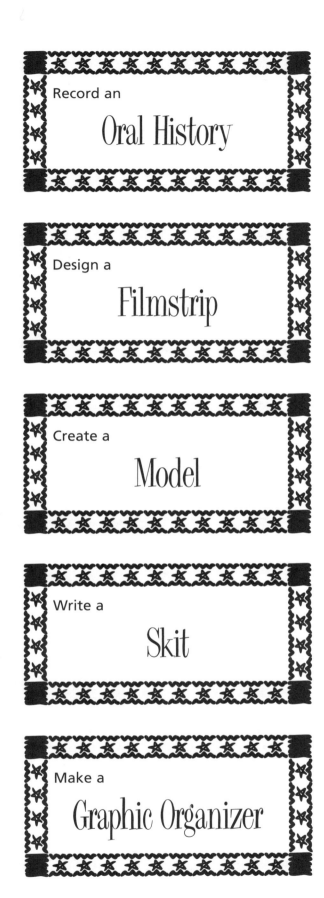

Record an
Oral History

Create a
Mobile

Design a
Filmstrip

Make a
Fact File

Create a
Model

Design a
Game

Write a
Skit

Create a
Crossword Puzzle

Make a
Graphic Organizer

Write a
Speech

31

Idea 3

Design a

Learning Center

Create a

Mural

Design a

Poster

Make an

Annotated Bibliography

Idea 3

Idea 4

Critical and Creative Thinking Skills

Although all students can benefit from learning critical and creative thinking skills, students who are gifted and talented can benefit at an earlier age and faster pace than most other students. When teaching these skills, you will want to make sure students understand the critical elements of the thinking skill. You also will want to provide students with opportunities to practice and to generalize the thinking skills to other situations.

Critical and creative thinking skills can be taught using several instructional arrangements. For example, you might choose to teach whole-group activities if you are teaching a self-contained class of gifted students. Teaching a small group or using learning centers are other instructional arrangements, particularly if gifted and talented students are in heterogeneously grouped classes. This idea provides examples of teaching and ways to categorize critical and creative thinking skills.

Teach a Whole-Group Lesson

Teach a whole-group lesson to the entire class using deductive (general to specific) or inductive (specific to general) reasoning.

Use the following steps to teach a thinking skill using **deductive reasoning**:

❶ Provide the definition and the critical elements of the skill.

❷ Practice the skill using one example.

❸ Provide students, either individually or in small groups, additional examples and nonexamples of the skill.

❹ Provide opportunities for students to practice and generalize the skill to other situations.

Use the following steps to teach a thinking skill using **inductive reasoning**:

❶ Complete several activities using the thinking skill.

❷ Define and generate the critical elements of the thinking skill (with the entire class).

❸ Provide students, either individually or in small groups, additional examples and nonexamples of the skill.

❹ Provide opportunities for students to practice and generalize the skill to other situations.

Teach a Small-Group Lesson

Divide the class into small groups (if in a classroom that uses cluster grouping of gifted students, place all the gifted students in a group). Give directions to the entire class or provide each group with a directions form. Use deductive or inductive reasoning, following the steps above.

Make a Center

Allow a student to access the center either in place of something the rest of the class is doing or when the student has completed other work (see Idea 5, Learning in Centers). Make sure the center is set up so the student can work independently. The teacher will want to follow these guidelines when setting up a center:

❶ Outline the goals and objective for the center.

❷ Collect the resources and materials necessary for students to complete these goals and objectives.

❸ Write clear directions and post them in a prominent place.

❹ Set a time limit for student participation in the center.

❺ Decide how you will evaluate the results of the student's work.

Example 1 (Whole-Group Lesson):
Finding Similarities and Differences

Materials Needed

- Example tasks of finding similarities and differences

- Nonexamples (other thinking skills)

- Overhead of Similarities/Differences T chart (provided on next page)

----

❶ Introduce the critical thinking skill of finding similarities and differences. Define the skill by stating that finding similarities between two ideas, objects, phenomena, and so on is to find characteristics in common, whereas finding differences is to find characteristics that distinguish ideas, and so on, from one another. Write the critical elements of this thinking skill where all students can see them. The critical elements are the following:

- Generate a list of significant characteristics.

- Categorize each characteristic as something that the ideas, objects, and so on have in common (similarity) or something that distinguishes one from the others (difference).

----

❷ Teach the lesson.

a. For younger students, find similarities and differences between two communities. For example, compare one class with another within your school, or compare one city with another within your state. For older students, find similarities and differences between two cultures.

b. Have the students generate an exhaustive list of characteristics (e.g., geographic location, climate, language, conflict, religion) and write them on the board or on chart paper.

c. Project the overhead of the T chart found on the next page. Read each characteristic aloud, and ask the students to categorize it as a similarity or difference. Write the characteristic in the correct column.

d. After the characteristics have been categorized, ask the students how the similarities and differences help them understand the relationship between the two communities or cultures.

e. Have the students complete one or more of the finding similarities/differences tasks that you have provided (examples) and compare this with other thinking skills, such as making inferences (nonexamples).

----

❸ Provide opportunities to practice the skill and generalize to other situations.

☞ **Tips:**

- Throughout the year, provide ample opportunities for students to generalize their knowledge of finding similarities and differences to many situations in different content areas.

- A blank T chart has been provided to use to teach other critical and creative thinking skills.

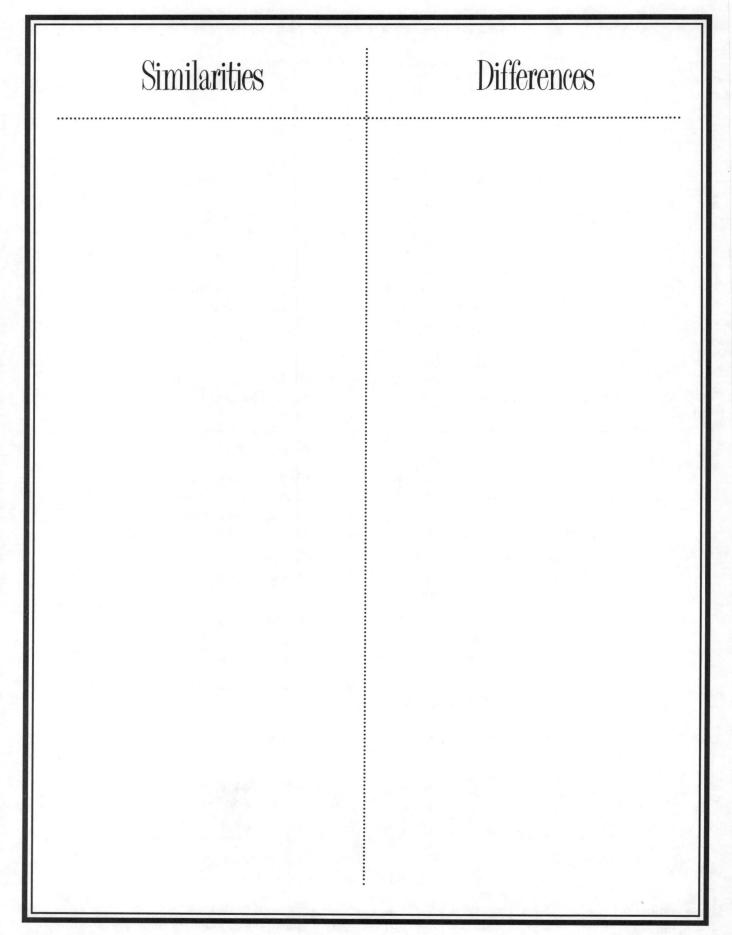

Similarities

Differences

Idea 4

37

Example 2 (Small-Group Lesson): Evaluation

Materials Needed

- A current problem or issue being studied or one that is important to the school

- A blank Evaluation Form for each group (provided at the end of this idea)

- Procedures and Completing the Evaluation Form cards (provided on the next page)

- Several additional worksheets or tasks using evaluation and nonexamples (give the same set to each group)

- Group Participation Evaluation forms (provided at the end of this idea)

----

❶ Divide the class into small groups, assigning each group a number. Show the Procedures and Completing the Evaluation Form cards on the overhead (or give each group its own card). Provide each group with the materials needed to complete the assignment. Use the Evaluation Form found with this idea or design your own.

----

❷ Have each group complete these steps.

a. Choose a problem or issue to address.

b. Direct each group to follow Steps 1 to 4 from the Procedures card.

c. After a specified time, have each group present its findings to the entire class.

d. Refine the critical elements of evaluation until all the groups are satisfied. Although there is no exact answer for the critical elements, students should include variations on the following:
   — List solutions or statements about a problem or issue
   — Generate five or more criteria or standards on which to judge the solutions or statements
   — Make judgments regarding the merits of solutions or statements based on their criteria or standards

e. Have each group member complete the Group Participation Evaluation form.

----

❸ Provide opportunities to practice the skill and generalize to other situations.

> ☞ **Tip:**
>
> Throughout the year, provide ample opportunities for students to generalize their knowledge of inferences to many situations in different content areas.

Procedures

❶ Choose a recorder and a spokesperson for the group.

❷ Complete an evaluation grid for your problem by following the directions for completing the Evaluation Form.

❸ Complete the examples and nonexamples provided to your group.

❹ Generate the critical elements of evaluation.

❺ Share the critical elements with the rest of the class.

❻ As a class, refine the critical elements until all groups are satisfied.

Completing the Evaluation Form

❶ Brainstorm several solutions to the problem and list these on the left side of the Evaluation Form in the spaces provided.

❷ Brainstorm a list of criteria by which to judge your solutions. Place the five most important criteria along the top of the grid in the spaces provided. If one criterion is twice as important as all the other criteria, list it twice.

❸ Rank order each solution based on each criterion and enter the rank in the blank.

❹ Add the ranks for each solution and find its average rank.

❺ The solution that has the lowest average rank will usually be your best solution.

Idea 4

Evaluation Form

Solutions								Total	Average

Group Participation Evaluation

Statement	Strongly Agree	Agree	Neutral	Disagree	Strongly Disagree
1. I did my fair share to complete our group's assignment.					
2. The members of my group worked well together.					
3. Our group was able to complete the assignment in the time allotted.					
4. I was satisfied with our group's final product.					
5. Working in a group was an effective way for me to learn this concept.					

Other Comments: _____

_____

_____

_____

_____

_____

41

Group Participation Evaluation

Statement	Yes	No
1. I did my part.	☺	☹
2. Everyone worked hard.	☺	☹
3. I liked our final project.	☺	☹
4. This was a good way for me to learn.	☺	☹

Group Participation Evaluation

Statement	Yes	No
1. I did my part.	☺	☹
2. Everyone worked hard.	☺	☹
3. I liked our final project.	☺	☹
4. This was a good way for me to learn.	☺	☹

Idea 4

Example 3 (Center): Attribute Listing

Materials Needed

- At least four or five problems appropriate for the age level of the student. For example, elementary students could work on improving the food served in the cafeteria. Secondary students could work on saving a species from extinction. Put the problems in a special folder.

- Example form (a completed form is provided)

- Several blank forms (a blank form is provided)

- Directions card for completing form (provided)

- Procedures card (provided)

- Several additional worksheets or tasks using attribute listing and nonexamples; place these in folders marked examples and nonexamples

- A quiet place for working

> ☞ **Tip:**
>
> Laminate the completed forms, the Directions card and the Procedures card and mount them on a divider.

❶ Find a commercially developed example of attribute listing or use the example Attribute Listing form found with this idea to create your own example. Complete at least one example and place in the center.

❷ Have the student complete the four tasks found on the Procedures card. Although there is no exact answer for the critical elements, students should include variations on the following:

- List general categories of a problem, issue, or system

- List the attributes of each category

- Identify ideas for improving each attribute

❸ Provide opportunities to practice the skill and generalize to other situations. Have the student present the finished product to the class or another appropriate audience.

> ☞ **Tip:**
>
> Provide opportunities to use attribute listing across content areas.

Note. The Attribute Listing form is adapted from "Fostering Creative Thinking" (pp. 399–444), by B. Cramond, in F. A. Karnes and S. M. Bean (Eds.), *Methods and Materials for Teaching the Gifted,* 2001, Waco, TX: Prufrock Press. Copyright 2001 by Prufrock Press. Adapted with permission.

Attribute Listing

Problem: _How can we improve the cafeteria food?_

Category	Attribute	Ideas for Improvement	Positive/Negative
Selection	• Not enough variety • One selection results in long line	Have several small snack bars, such as a hamburger bar, a salad bar, and a sandwich bar	The lines would be shorter at each snack bar / It would be costly to have servers and cooks for so many different foods
Cost	• Too high	Use volunteers to serve the food	Food service would be free / It might be difficult to find enough volunteers
Location	• Too small • No ambience	Eat outside on nice days	Students could choose to eat in or out, which would reduce the crowding, and it would be more pleasant / Trash may be left outside
Noise	• Too loud	Use smaller round tables	Students could talk together more easily and noise level would be reduced / Too many students might crowd around one table

Idea 4

Attribute Listing

Problem: _____

Category	Attribute	Ideas for Improvement	Positive/Negative

45

Idea 4

Procedures

1. Choose one problem and complete one or more of the Attribute Listing forms. See the examples and the Directions card for completing the forms.

2. Choose two examples and nonexamples from the folders and complete the tasks.

3. Generate the critical elements of attribute listing.

4. Make a poster, overhead, or another product showing the critical elements of attribute listing to share with the rest of the class.

Idea 4

Directions for Completing the Attribute Listing Form

1. Choose one problem from the problem folder.

2. List several of the categories of the problem in column 1.

3. List attributes of each category in column 2.

4. Develop one or more ideas for improving the attribute in column 3.

5. Write at least one positive feature and one negative feature of the idea for improvement in column 4.

Idea 4

Directions: Write the procedures the student is to follow on the first card and the directions for using forms you develop for the center on the second card. Laminate these and place them in the center.

Procedures

Idea 4

Directions

Sampling of Critical and Creative Thinking Skills

Bloom. There are several ways to categorize thinking skills; probably the most familiar to educators is Bloom's taxonomy.

✗ *Knowledge* (Remember information or processes)

✗ *Comprehension* (Interpret, extrapolate, and translate events or information)

✗ *Application* (Use principles, concepts, theories, generalizations to solve problems or apply them in new situations)

✗ *Analysis* (Dissect, detect elements, or see relationships among parts)

✗ *Synthesis* (Combine or integrate concepts, principles, or information into unified whole)

✗ *Evaluation* (Make judgments using standards or criteria)

Paul. Richard Paul (1990) identified 35 dimensions of critical thinking, 9 of which he classified as the microskills of cognitive strategies. We have paraphrased them as the following:

❧ *Distinguish between facts and ideals* (Recognize gaps between what is fact and what are ideals)

❧ *Think precisely about thinking* (Make thinking better, more clear, more accurate, and more fair)

❧ *Finding similarities and differences* (Make discriminating comparisons)

❧ *Examine or evaluate assumptions* (Question assumptions and consider alternate assumptions)

❧ *Distinguish relevant from irrelevant facts* (Recognize that a fact is only relevant or irrelevant in relation to an issue)

❧ *Make inferences, predictions, or interpretations* (Reach sound judgments based on observation and information)

❧ *Evaluate evidence* (Take reasoning apart and examine and evaluate its components)

❧ *Recognize contradictions* (Recognize where opposing arguments or viewpoints contradict each other)

❧ *Explore implications and consequences* (Recognize implications of statements and develop a complete understanding of their meaning)

Torrance. Torrance used the following terms to define divergent productions.

◆ *Fluency* (Recall or think of a number of ideas)

◆ *Flexibility* (Produce new ideas that deviate from expected ideas or that shift categorically during the idea-producing process)

◆ *Originality* (Synthesize ideas into a new or unique whole; develop novel ideas)

◆ *Elaboration* (Fill in details or develop ideas more fully)

Ennis. Ennis (1962) developed three types of thinking skills:

✿ *Define and clarify* (Identify central issues and problems, conclusions, reasons, questions, and assumptions)

✿ *Judge information* (Determine credibility and relevance; recognize consistency)

✿ *Infer, solve problems, and draw reasonable conclusions* (Judge inductive conclusions and deductive validity; predict probable consequences)

Research-Based Creative Thinking Skills.

★ *Brainstorming* (Produce as many ideas as possible)

★ *SCAMPER* (Substitute, Combine, Adjust, Modify: Magnify or Minify, Put to Other Uses, Eliminate, Reverse or Rearrange) (see Idea 1)

★ *Synectics* (Use analogies to solve problems: direct—make comparisons with similar situations; personal—the problem solver identifies with some aspect of the problem; symbolic—use objective and impersonal image to represent problem or put two conflicting aspects of the problem together; fantasy—use imaginary ideas to find solutions)

★ *Attribute listing* (List categories of characteristics)

★ *Morphological analysis or checkerboarding* (List attributes from one dimension along the top and attributes of another dimension along the side; combine the attributes of both dimensions in the cells of the grid)

★ *Morphological synthesis* (List the attributes of the situation; below each attribute brainstorm many alternatives, combine alternatives from different columns)

★ *Forced relationships* (Make two dissimilar things relate to one another)

References. Ennis, R. H. (1962). A concept of critical thinking. *Harvard Educational Review, 32,* 81–111.

Paul, R. W. (1990). *Critical thinking: What every person needs to survive in a rapidly changing world.* Rohnert, CA: Center for Critical Thinking and Moral Critique.

Torrance, E. P., & White, W. F. (Eds). (1966). *Issues and advances in education psychology.* Istica, IL: F. E. Peacock.

Idea 5

Learning in Centers

Teachers have used learning centers for many years. This type of instruction, which involves active student involvement in learning tasks that are planned and prepared in advance, is a great alternative to direct instruction. Learning centers can be established in specific areas of the classroom and used to

- teach something new,

- provide enrichment,

- clarify concepts, and

- motivate.

There are several ways to organize learning centers.

❶ Specific skills (classification, listening for meaning, brainstorming)

❷ Student interests (robotics, music, mythology)

❸ In-depth study (particular topic such as the Civil War)

❹ Thematic units (using many content areas to teach generalizations)

Activity Examples

Specific Skills: Listening for Meaning

✘ Listening to an audiotape of a lecture only once, then identifying key points

✘ Identifying objects in closed boxes by shaking them

✘ Examining background noise: What is it? How was it first used? What impact does it have?

✘ Listening to musical selections or audiobooks with and without headphones; then contrasting the two experiences

✘ Identifying specific behaviors that indicate to most people that you are listening carefully

✘ Preparing an instructional videotape that teaches students how to listen for meaning

Student Interests: Music

✪ Analyzing different styles of musical selections available on CDs, including pop, R & B, jazz, salsa, and classical

✪ Writing a compare–contrast paper that examines two famous musicians in the same genre (e.g., John Lennon and Mick Jagger)

✪ Drawing a poster that emphasizes positive aspects of a particular musician

✪ Designing original art for a CD cover

In-depth Study: Civil War

✤ Preparing a PowerPoint presentation of the major causes of the Civil War

✤ Writing a journal from two points of view: as a Confederate soldier and as a Yankee soldier

✤ Analyzing the Gettysburg Address

✤ Evaluating the Supreme Court's decision in the Dred Scott case

Thematic Unit: Power

◆ Writing a persuasive essay that addresses controversial issues involving powerful institutions (e.g., courts, the media, the wealthy) (language arts)

◆ Solving math problems that include different powers of numbers (math)

◆ Making a mask of a powerful figure that emphasizes specific features or attributes (art)

◆ Identifying powerful companies and how they became powerful (social studies)

◆ Describing powerful forces of nature like hurricanes and tornadoes (science)

Here are the basic steps for creating a learning center.

❶ Decide what you hope to accomplish. This can be something new you want to teach (making mathematical conjectures), something in which you want to provide enrichment (number bases), or an area that needs to be reinforced (math estimation).

❷ Write the name and the objectives of the center and post them in the center (e.g., Math Estimation: In this center, students will learn more about math estimation by (a) identifying key information in math problems, (b) deciding on the purpose of math problems, (c) restating the rules for estimation, (d) completing a variety of math estimation problems, and (e) checking your math work).

❸ Develop learning center activities; provide the materials and equipment to complete the activities (e.g., audiotapes, videotapes, books and articles, art supplies, worksheets, a computer with Internet access and various software programs, poster board, manipulatives, overhead acetates, tape recorder); write clear directions for using them.

❹ Contract with students about when they can use the learning center (e.g., instead of work they have already mastered).

❺ Create a log for monitoring the activities students complete. We have provided three record forms: one for multiple centers, one for single centers, and one for young students.

❻ Provide feedback and evaluate the final product (e.g., student makes a class presentation and completes a self-evaluation).

Record Form for Multiple Centers

Name _____

Fill in the date under the day you complete the objectives for each center.

Center	Monday	Tuesday	Wednesday	Thursday	Friday
1.					
2.					
3.					
4.					

Final Product for Each Center

Center 1: _____

Center 2: _____

Center 3: _____

Center 4: _____

One Thing I Learned from Each Center

Center 1: _____

Center 2: _____

Center 3: _____

Center 4: _____

Signatures

Teacher _____   Date _____

Student _____   Date _____

Idea 5

Record Form for One Center

Name _____

Week of _____

Center _____

Check off the activities you completed each day this week.

Activity	Monday	Tuesday	Wednesday	Thursday	Friday
1.					
2.					
3.					
4.					

Teacher Evaluation and Feedback

Activity 1: _____

Activity 2: _____

Activity 3: _____

Activity 4: _____

My Final Product

_____

What I Learned from Participating in This Center

_____

Signatures

Teacher _____   Date _____

Student _____   Date _____

Idea 5

 # Learning Center
Magic

Name _____ Date _____

Activities to Complete _____

Complete this contract for a magical experience.

	Activities	Materials	✓ Completed
Centers	1.		
	2.		
	3.		
	1.		
	2.		
	3.		
	1.		
	2.		
	3.		

Idea 6
Design a WebQuest

Using the Internet is a motivating teaching tool because most students enjoy searching the Web. Gifted children, in particular, are curious and love to discover things. Very young children can conduct research projects if they are set up correctly. This idea provides a method for setting up a WebQuest.

Here are the steps to set up a WebQuest.

❶ *Write the objectives of the lesson.*
Refer back to these objectives when designing your WebQuest.

❷ *Find Web sites that address your objectives.*
Include each site's URL so students will spend less time in random searching and more time on the objectives of the project.

❸ *Write an introduction to the WebQuest.*
Write one paragraph that contains the main objective of the project; it should be written as a simulation or as an advanced organizer.

❹ *Outline the process.*
Address to the students and make a list of the steps that must be completed.

❺ *Design an evaluation.*
This is usually a rubric (see Idea 19, Develop a Rubric).

❻ *Write a conclusion.*
Wrap up the loose ends for the students and summarize what has been learned or accomplished.

❼ *Test the project and revise as needed.*

☞ **Tips:**
If your students are familiar with using the Internet and have had a lot of experience with independent studies, provide a common pool of Web sites and let them choose among them.

You may also provide print materials for students.

⇨ We have included a form to use when designing your WebQuest or you can design your WebQuest online by visiting the following sites:

webquest.sdsu.edu/webquest.html

www.ozline.com

sesd.sk.ca/teacherresource

school.discovery.com/schrockguide/webquest/webquest.html

WebQuest Planner

Topic _Global Warming_

Introduction _You are a group of young scientists chosen to present your findings on the impact of global warming to your country's government. You will:_

Objectives

1. Define global warming.
2. Decide if there is sufficient evidence that global warming is a problem for your region.
3. List major causes and find solutions.
4. Choose one solution and develop implementation strategies.

Web Resources

URL	Brief Description	Objective Number
www.epa.gov/globalwarming/impacts/index.html	Defines global warming/presents causes	2
globalwarming.enviroweb.org	Impact of gw /now and future	1, 3
climatehotmap.org	Impact of gw on areas of earth	2
www.climateclub.org/globalwarming	Solutions to gw	3, 4
www.sierraclub.org/globalwarming	Comprehensive gw Web page developed by concerned scientists	1, 2, 3, 4
www.ucsusa.org/warming	FAQs about greenhouse effect	1, 2, 3
archive.greenpeace.org/~climate/climatefaq.html		

Other Resources

Name of Article/Book/Other	Brief Description	Objective Number
Global Warming	Examines causes and consequences	2, 3, 4
Acting for Nature	Stories of young people tackling environmental issues	4
Greenhouse	History of global warming	1, 2

Process

Step 1: _Define global warming._
Step 2: _Create a map, label and give causes of global warming._
Step 3: _Select one major cause of global warming to focus on and research solutions._
Step 4: _Use backwards brainstorming to choose one solution on which to focus._
Step 5: _Develop implementation plan for solution._
Step 6: _Prepare PowerPoint presentation._

WebQuest Planner

Topic _____

Introduction _____

_____

_____

Objectives

1. _____
2. _____
3. _____
4. _____

Web Resources

URL	Brief Description	Objective Number

Other Resources

Name of Article/Book/Other	Brief Description	Objective Number

Process

Step 1: _____

Step 2: _____

Step 3: _____

Step 4: _____

Step 5: _____

Step 6: _____

Idea 6

Idea 7
Diagnostic–Prescriptive Method

Students who are gifted in a particular academic subject will resist doing work that they have already mastered. Many of these students will develop behavior problems, others will tune out.

Teachers can provide appropriate challenge if they use a diagnostic–prescriptive approach. This method *diagnoses* what the student has mastered in the upcoming curriculum and *prescribes* the appropriate curriculum for the student. One excellent diagnostic–prescriptive method developed by Joseph Renzulli and Linda H. Smith is called the Compactor. A filled-in example and a blank form are provided.

Here's how it works.

❶ Identify the standards or objectives in the upcoming curriculum and write them in the first column of the form.

❷ Pretest the student on each objective or standard. Record the pretest method in column 2 and results in column 3 of the form.

❸ Develop alternatives to the regular curriculum and record them in column 4. Alternatives include enrichment and acceleration. Enrichment involves studying a topic in depth; acceleration speeds up the curriculum. For example, a student might contract to do an independent study in a topic (enrichment) or may move on to the next standard or objective that he or she has not already mastered (acceleration).

❹ Keep records by writing the date the student has completed the alternative in column 4.

Note. The Compactor is adapted from *The Compactor,* by J. S. Renzulli and L. H. Smith, 1975, Mansfield Center, CT: Creative Learning Press. Copyright 1975 by Creative Learning Press. Adapted with permission.

The Compactor

Name _Rachelle Thompson_

Subject Area _mathematics_

Date _Oct. 15_

Standard/Objective	Pretest	Results	Alternative Assignment	Completion Date
1. Describe measures of central tendency.	End of unit test	93% accuracy	Rachelle will develop a survey on topic of interest. She will collect, analyze, display, and interpret survey information. She will report measures of central tendency and display results using graphical method of her choice. Final product will be poster of her method, results, and interpretation.	Nov. 25
2. Interpret data from a variety of graphical methods.	Teacher developed problems interpreting information from histogram, pie chart, and line graphs.	100% accuracy		
			Meet with mentor on Friday afternoon to explore advanced mathematical topics.	

☞ Tip:

If using a textbook as a curriculum guide, use the unit tests as pretests.

The Compactor

Name _____

Subject Area _____

Date _____

Standard/Objective	Pretest	Results	Alternative Assignment	Completion Date

Idea 8

Contracting

Students who are gifted and talented need opportunities to study a topic in more depth than other students. The focus of in-depth study should be on inquiry rather than memorization. You can contract with a student for him or her to find out what, how, and how long. We have included three sample contracts. The first can be used with elementary students, the second with intermediate students, and the third with secondary students.

Here are some important considerations.

❶ Ensure that the student has mastered the basic concepts.

❷ Provide experiences that will assist the student in understanding the big picture by integrating facts and knowledge with synthesis and analysis.

❸ Assist students in obtaining the tools they need to complete the inquiry.

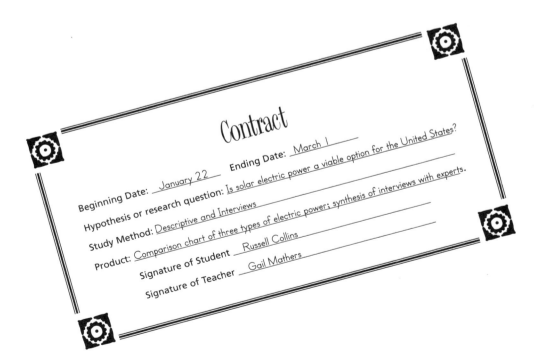

Contract

Beginning Date: _January 22_   Ending Date: _March 1_

Hypothesis or research question: _Is solar electric power a viable option for the United States?_

Study Method: _Descriptive and Interviews_

Product: _Comparison chart of three types of electric power; synthesis of interviews with experts._

Signature of Student _Russell Collins_

Signature of Teacher _Gail Mathers_

Contract

I will learn more about _____.

I will begin on _____ and finish on _____.

(beginning date)   (ending date)

I need help to do the following:

What	Who Will Help	Initials
_____	_____	_____
_____	_____	_____
_____	_____	_____
_____	_____	_____

I will complete these steps:

1. _____.
2. _____.
3. _____.
4. _____.

My final product will be:

_____

Signature of Student _____

Signature of Teacher _____

Idea 8

Contract

My inquiry will answer this question:

_____

Beginning Date of Inquiry _____ Ending Date of Inquiry _____

I will complete the following steps to answer my question:

1. _____

   _____

2. _____

   _____

3. _____

   _____

4. _____

   _____

Final Product _____

      Signature of Student _____

      Signature of Teacher _____

Idea 8

Contract

Beginning Date _____   Ending Date _____

Hypothesis or Research Question _____

Study Method _____

Product _____

       Signature of Student _____

       Signature of Teacher _____

Contract

Beginning Date _____   Ending Date _____

Hypothesis or Research Question _____

Study Method _____

Product _____

       Signature of Student _____

       Signature of Teacher _____

Idea 8

Idea 9

Accelerate

In Idea 7, Diagnostic–Prescriptive Method, we provided a way to accelerate students through the curriculum. This idea, on the other hand, helps you determine when and if a student should be accelerated an entire grade or more. Macroacceleration or grade skipping is a controversial issue for some educators and parents. Their biggest concern is the negative effect macroacceleration might have on a student's social and emotional development. There exists, however, a body of research that suggests it is far better to accelerate students who are academically and emotionally ready than to keep them in their current grade because of age.

Accelerate focuses on skipping an entire grade, although educators may use it (along with information from Idea 7) to determine whether a child should be accelerated in a single subject.

Here are some general guidelines.

❶ Accelerating students when they are younger is better.

❷ Accelerate students at the beginning of the school year when possible.

❸ Accelerate with caution before a transition year (e.g., fourth grade [elementary] to sixth grade [middle school]).

❹ Acceleration is not a good option if a student will be placed in a sibling's grade.

❺ Acceleration requires the support of the receiving teacher, the administration, the parents, and the student.

On the next page, we provide a form that will guide you in making a decision to macroaccelerate. After you complete the form, decide what additional information you need to assist you in making your decision. Remember, the decision to accelerate should be a team effort and must take into account information from many sources.

Note. Educators desiring a more in-depth approach are referred to the *Iowa Acceleration Scale* by Susan Assouline, Nicholas Colangelo, Ann Lupkowski-Shoplik, and Jonathon Lipscomb, 1998, published by Gifted Psychology Press.

Student Name _____ Present Grade _____ Proposed Grade _____

➤Mark the accommodations that have already been made for the student.
  ❑ Participates in gifted program   ❑ Works with a mentor
  ❑ Receives enrichment in one or more   ❑ Completed one or more independent studies
    academic areas   in area of interest
  ❑ Accelerated in one or more subject areas ❑ Other _____

➤Is there an indication that the student needs additional accommodations than those marked above?
  ❑ Yes   ❑ No

➤Are there other accommodations that should be made before acceleration is considered?
  ❑ Yes   ❑ No
  If yes, what are they? _____

➤Mark the areas in which the student has demonstrated high or advanced ability as compared with age peers.
  ❑ Reading   ❑ Social Studies
  ❑ Language Arts   ❑ Foreign Language
  ❑ English   ❑ Other _____
  ❑ Science

➤List the names and scores of any standardized test (e.g., intelligence, ability, achievement).

Name of Test	Type of Score	Score
_____	_____	_____
_____	_____	_____
_____	_____	_____

➤Circle the appropriate response to the questions below. If you circle "No" to any of the questions, please attach an explanation.

Does the student enjoy rigorous academic work?	Yes	No	NA
Does the student complete most of his or her work quickly with few or no mistakes?	Yes	No	NA
Has the student already mastered much of the grade level material you are teaching?	Yes	No	NA
Does the student prefer to be with older students and/or adults?	Yes	No	NA
Does the student appear to be emotionally and socially older than his or her age peers?	Yes	No	NA
Does the student have the desire to accelerate to the next grade?	Yes	No	NA
Do you have the support of the receiving teacher?	Yes	No	NA
Do you have the support of the parents?	Yes	No	NA

➤Other areas taken into consideration:
  _____   _____
  _____   _____

➤Decision of the committee:
  Accelerate to grade _____
  Keep in current grade with the following accommodations: _____
  _____
  _____

Idea 9

Idea 10

Questions and Answers

When reviewing information with students, it is important to keep your questions challenging, interesting, and fun so they don't tune you out. Here are two quick and easy ways to keep students engaged and make sure that their level of comprehension is satisfactory.

In Other Words

After you ask a question, but before the student answers it, ask him or her to restate the question in his or her own words. Model for your students the first few times, and then build the restatement into your questioning sequence as a required step. This process will help students understand your question while giving them a chance to think of the answer on their own. For example, "What is the theme of *Gulliver's Travels*?" could be restated by the student as, "What is one lesson that the author of *Gulliver's Travels* was trying to teach?" It might help to use a 1-2-3 signal with your fingers:

❶ Listen to the question.

❷ Restate the question in your own words.

❸ Answer the question.

1 2 3

If No One Gets It but You, Then You Get It

One way to challenge students at the end of a lesson is to require them to write their own review questions, then call on other students to answer them. To motivate students even more, provide a special reward for students who can "stump" their classmates. Extra credit points, a free homework pass, an extra trip to the computer lab or library, or time to listen to music—any of these would be a great incentive for students. You might need to set some guidelines so that students don't make up ridiculously difficult questions just to earn the goodies. For example, you might want to require students to ask questions based on written material or discussion notes. However, be careful not to stifle their creativity.

For stumping your classmates, you have earned:

A free pass: No homework

For challenging your classmates, you have earned:

Automatic A on a quiz

For stumping your classmates, you have earned:

1 free correct answer on a test

For challenging your classmates, you have earned:

3 extra points on assignment of your choice

For stumping your classmates, you have earned:

1 hour in the library

For challenging your classmates, you have earned:

1 hour extra computer time

For stumping your classmates, you have earned:

_____

For challenging your classmates, you have earned:

_____

74

Idea 10

Idea 11

Beat the Pro

Here's a great way to review information and challenge your students while having fun. Beat the Pro is fast paced and sure to work with secondary students who like to prove to the teacher how much they know.

Here's how it works.

❶ After completing a section of reading or instruction, write an odd number of true–false statements about the content. (Probably 9 to 15 statements is a good range—not too many or the activity will take too long and bog down your instruction.)

❷ Present the statements to students on the board, an overhead, or a handout. Quickly read each statement and have the students raise their hands and vote on whether they think the statement is true or false.

❸ The answer that receives the majority of votes is the one that counts. If students are correct, they get a point. If they are incorrect, the Pro (the teacher) gets a point.

❹ Whoever has the most points after completing the review wins the game.

We have some ideas for prizes for your secondary students if they win. You can really have fun with this idea if you hype it up and get your students excited about beating you.

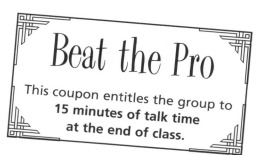

Note. Idea provided by and used with permission of David Carpenter, social studies teacher, Mountain View High School, Oren, Utah.

Beat the Pro

This coupon entitles the group to
**skip half of the
homework assignment.**

Beat the Pro

This coupon entitles the group to
**15 minutes of talk time
at the end of class.**

Beat the Pro

This coupon entitles the group to
**listen to music or a story
on tape.**

Beat the Pro

This coupon entitles the group to
no homework tonight.

Beat the Pro

This coupon entitles the group to
a free video rental.

Beat the Pro

This coupon entitles the group to
popcorn or candy.

Beat the Pro

This coupon entitles the group to
go to lunch 5 minutes early.

Beat the Pro

This coupon entitles the group to
**two bonus points on the
next quiz.**

Beat the Pro

This coupon entitles the group to
extra time in the library.

Beat the Pro

This coupon entitles the group to
listen to music.

Beat the Pro

This coupon entitles the group to
_____

Beat the Pro

This coupon entitles the group to
_____

Idea 11

Beat the Pro Prizes

☐   Talk time at the end of class

☐   No homework tonight

☐   Bonus points on your class average

☐   Have class outside during nice weather

☐   Bring a soft drink or bottle of water to class

☐   Popcorn or candy for everyone

☐   Teacher makes dessert for the class

☐   Music during work time

☐   Reading time (magazines or books)

☐   Video (class chooses, teacher approves)

☐   Friday cookies

☐   Drop two questions on next quiz

Idea 12

Easy as Pie, Tough as Nails

Almost all teachers are familiar with Bloom's Taxonomy, which organizes learning tasks in a hierarchy, from basic knowledge and comprehension to application, analysis, synthesis, and evaluation. It is important that teachers include questions at all of the taxonomy levels when they evaluate students' learning. Here is an easy-to-use format for writing questions. Use the Easy as Pie cards to construct questions that address low-level learning, then write Tough as Nails questions to determine whether students can answer higher level questions. The cards make it easy to remember to include a wide variety of questions in your plans.

☞ **Tip:**

To involve students actively in review and comprehension checks, require them to write their own questions. See if they can write at least one question for each card in both the easy and the tough category. You can then compile students' questions and use them on quizzes, in oral reviews, or for homework.

Who _____ _____ _____ _____?

What _____ _____ _____?

When _____ _____ _____?

Where _____ _____ _____?

Why _____ _____ _____?

How _____ _____ _____?

Idea 12

How do you feel about

_____

_____

_____ **?**

What can you infer

_____

_____

_____ **?**

Do you think

_____

_____

_____ **?**

How are _____

and _____

different?

What if

_____

_____

_____ **?**

What evidence do you

have for _____

_____

_____

_____ **?**

81

Idea 13

Socratic Starters

Socratic questioning is designed to address the underlying logic and structure of our thinking so that we can make reasonable judgments. According to Paul (1990), there are six kinds of Socratic questions. These are designed to:

1. Clarify

2. Probe assumptions

3. Probe reason and evidence

4. Examine viewpoints or perspectives

5. Probe implications and consequences

6. Question the question

When Socratic questions are used effectively, they can stimulate exploration and inquiry among students. Hopefully, good questions lead to more questions, so that students go beyond the recall of basic information and challenge. We have provided Socratic Starter question cards in each of the six areas.

Here are some ways to use them.

❶ Paste a question from each category on the cube template and make a die. Roll the die so that you prompt yourself to use the questions during discussions.

❷ When designing and planning lessons, choose one category of questions (e.g., questions to clarify) and focus the discussion on that specific type of question. Specific categories of questions will fit naturally with some specific content areas.

Note. This idea is adapted from *Critical Thinking: What Every Person Needs to Survive in a Rapidly Changing World,* by R. W. Paul, 1990, Rohnert Park, CA: Center for Critical Thinking and Moral Critique. Copyright 1990 by Center for Critical Thinking and Moral Critique. www.criticalthinking.org. Adapted with permission.

❸ Pass out the Socratic Starter questions to small groups of students. After reading a passage of content information or completing a lecture, ask each group to use the questions as guides for a discussion among members of the group.

❹ Line up questions from each category and ask students to write a short paragraph that answers the questions. Tell them to put them into logical order and make sure the questions fit the content.

☞ Tips:

- Avoid yes–no questions.

- Avoid the question, "Do you understand?" and replace with a statement like, "Give me an example so I know you understand."

- Use both open-ended and closed questions, as well as clarifying questions.

- Allow enough wait time for students to think. They need to consider the question as well as their response.

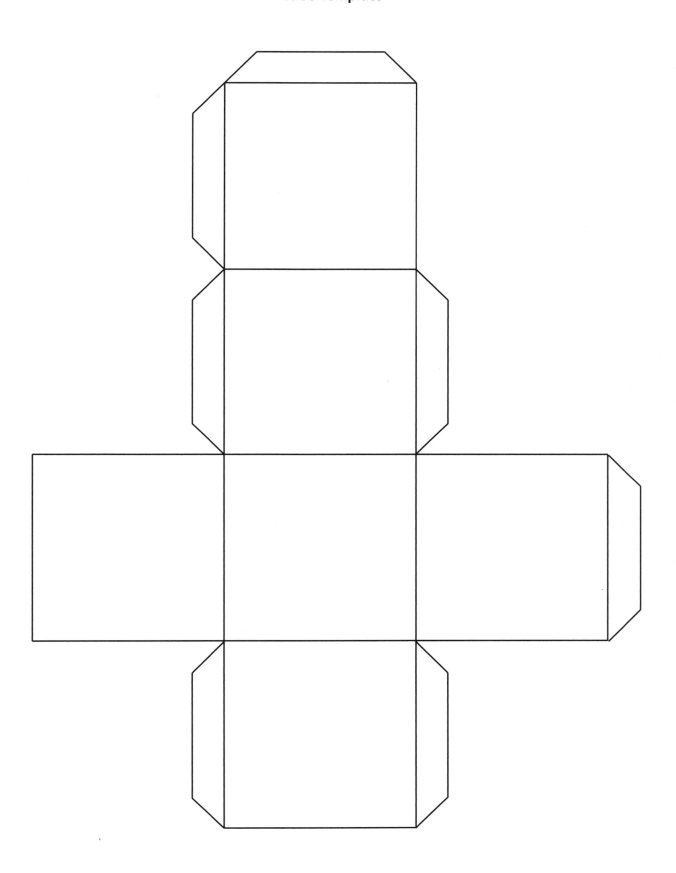

What do you mean by _____?

How does _____ relate to _____?

How does what you said relate to what _____ just said?

What is your key point?

How else might you say that?

Could you explain your point further?

What do you think is the most important issue?

What is an example of that?

Why do you say _____?

Would you summarize what _____ just said?

Note. This idea is adapted from *Critical Thinking: What Every Person Needs to Survive in a Rapidly Changing World,* by R. W. Paul, 1990, Rohnert Park, CA: Center for Critical Thinking and Moral Critique. Copyright 1990 by Center for Critical Thinking and Moral Critique. www.criticalthinking.org. Adapted with permission.

Idea 13

What are you assuming?

What is _____ assuming?

Why have you based your reasoning on _____ rather than on _____?

Why are you assuming _____?

Give me an example of when your assumption would not be correct.

Why would somebody assume _____?

What could we assume instead?

You seem to be assuming _____. How do you justify your position?

Note. This idea is adapted from *Critical Thinking: What Every Person Needs to Survive in a Rapidly Changing World,* by R. W. Paul, 1990, Rohnert Park, CA: Center for Critical Thinking and Moral Critique. Copyright 1990 by Center for Critical Thinking and Moral Critique. www.criticalthinking.org. Adapted with permission.

Idea 13

Questions To Probe Reason and Evidence

What would be an example of _____?

Why do you think you are right?

Can you explain your reasons to us?

Why do you think it is an example of _____?

What led you to that belief?

Are your reasons adequate to make that conclusion?

How does that example apply to this situation?

What would make you change your mind?

Is there evidence to support that conclusion?

What are your reasons for saying that?

Note. This idea is adapted from *Critical Thinking: What Every Person Needs to Survive in a Rapidly Changing World*, by R. W. Paul, 1990, Rohnert Park, CA: Center for Critical Thinking and Moral Critique. Copyright 1990 by Center for Critical Thinking and Moral Critique. www.criticalthinking.org. Adapted with permission.

Idea 13

Questions To Examine Viewpoints or Perspectives

If someone were to disagree with you, what would they say?

What is another way of saying that?

How do you think _____ would feel about that?

Why might someone disagree?

How are _____'s ideas and _____'s alike?

What do you think _____ would say about your position?

What is an alternative point of view?

How are _____'s ideas and _____'s different?

If someone disagreed with you, how would you try to convince them of your position?

Note. This idea is adapted from *Critical Thinking: What Every Person Needs to Survive in a Rapidly Changing World,* by R. W. Paul, 1990, Rohnert Park, CA: Center for Critical Thinking and Moral Critique. Copyright 1990 by Center for Critical Thinking and Moral Critique. www.criticalthinking.org. Adapted with permission.

Idea 13

Questions To Probe Implications and Consequences

When you say _____, what are you implying?

Can you imply that because _____ happened once, it will happen again? Why?

Is _____ an effect of _____? Why?

Why are you implying _____?

How is your implication a consequence of _____?

What might be the consequence of doing that?

If you imply _____, what is the consequence?

If _____ happened, what else might happen? Why?

Note. This idea is adapted from *Critical Thinking: What Every Person Needs to Survive in a Rapidly Changing World,* by R. W. Paul, 1990, Rohnert Park, CA: Center for Critical Thinking and Moral Critique. Copyright 1990 by Center for Critical Thinking and Moral Critique. www.criticalthinking.org. Adapted with permission.

Idea 13

Questions About the Question

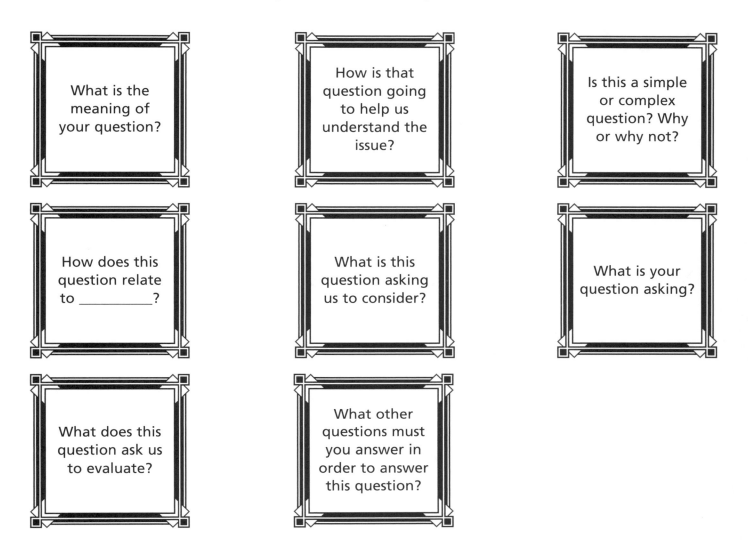

What is the meaning of your question?

How is that question going to help us understand the issue?

Is this a simple or complex question? Why or why not?

How does this question relate to _____?

What is this question asking us to consider?

What is your question asking?

What does this question ask us to evaluate?

What other questions must you answer in order to answer this question?

Note. This idea is adapted from *Critical Thinking: What Every Person Needs to Survive in a Rapidly Changing World,* by R. W. Paul, 1990, Rohnert Park, CA: Center for Critical Thinking and Moral Critique. Copyright 1990 by Center for Critical Thinking and Moral Critique. www.criticalthinking.org. Adapted with permission.

Idea 13

Idea 14

Socratic Discussion

The previous idea provides general Socratic questioning strategies. This idea takes it a step further and provides a discussion technique to use to focus on a specific issue. This allows you to probe the issue in depth and helps students clarify their thoughts and perspectives.

Here are general suggestions to follow for a good Socratic Discussion.

❶ Require all students to read and research all pertinent material before the discussion takes place.

❷ Sit in a circle so all students can make eye contact.

❸ Allow the discussion to flow on its own.

❹ Allow each student at least one opportunity to pass during the discussion.

The teacher's role is to act as the facilitator. As the facilitator you:

◆ Enforce discipline in the discussion.

◆ Remind students that every comment is given due consideration.

◆ Stop students from interrupting or making rude comments to someone who has the floor.

◆ Ask a different student an open-ended question if one person is dominating the discussion.

◆ Periodically summarize the discussion and remind the students what questions are still unanswered.

◆ Construct a list of main questions to be addressed.

To construct a main list of questions, begin with the main questions and then pose additional questions you would have to answer in order to answer the first ones. Continue this process until you have a list of questions relevant to the first questions.

We have provided two forms of the general guidelines for a good Socratic Discussion for you to copy, laminate, and post in your room (or make an overhead transparency).

Here's an example.

➤ *Suppose one of the big questions you want to answer is*

Don't many examples of Keats's poetry contradict his concept of negative capability?

➤ *Relevant questions might be*

- How do you think Keats would define negative capability?

- How would you define negative capability?

- What are some examples of Keats's poetry that illustrate negative capability?

- How do these examples illustrate the concept?

- What are some examples of Keats's poetry that contradict negative capability?

- How do these examples contradict this concept?

- How would you compare negative capability to sentimentalism?

- Who are other poets who would agree with Keats's concept of negative capability?

- Why would they agree?

- Who are other poets who would disagree with Keats's concept of negative capability?

- Why would they disagree?

- What evidence do you have to support this assertion?

☞ Tip:

Use an inner–outer circle strategy. In this technique you place students in two concentric circles. The inner circle discusses the issue. The outer circle listens, takes notes, and discusses the discussion.

General Guidelines for a Socratic Discussion

➤ Support all answers with evidence.

➤ Speak to one another (not the facilitator).

➤ Use active listening.

➤ Respect the comments of others.

➤ Be honest with your opinion.

General Guidelines for a Socratic Discussion

◉ Tell why you think your answer is good.

◉ Talk to the other students, not the teacher.

◉ Listen.

◉ Respect each other.

◉ Be honest.

Idea 14

Idea 15

Outline Line

Most students benefit when teachers provide them with cues for focussing during instruction and for remembering what they have learned after instruction. Here's an idea for using graphic organizers that has a new twist: The organizers are not provided as a pencil and paper outline for students, they are displayed one at a time in a line across the classroom.

Here's how to use the Outline Line idea.

❶ Before beginning your direct instruction, prepare signs or small posters that contain the key words, phrases, dates, names, or other facts from the reading. Make the posters bright, clearly visible, and engaging by adding logos or borders or using colored paper. Generally, 11″ × 14″ signs are easy to see and not too cumbersome.

❷ Prepare to display your posters by either stringing a clothesline across the room or clearing a wall. If you use a clothesline, you will need clothespins to attach your posters and signs; if you choose to use a wall, put sticky putty or double-sided tape on the back of each poster.

❸ As you begin to teach the lesson, hang up the first sign or poster. This could be a key word or phrase, a picture, a humorous cartoon, or a few bulleted phrases designed to tell your students the key topic or objective of the lesson.

Note. This idea is adapted from *TNT Teaching: Over 200 Dynamite Ways to Make Your Classroom Come Alive,* by R. Moberg, 1994, Minneapolis, MN: Free Spirit, 800/735-7323, www.freespirit.com. Copyright 1994 by Randy Moberg. Adapted with permission.

❹ As you continue your instruction, stop frequently to hang up additional signs or posters one at a time. You also can add concrete objects. These props will focus students' attention and give them cues to help them remember the content.

❺ When the lesson is over, ask students to restate the key points, elaborate with details, or ask questions about what they have learned. If your classroom is large enough to accommodate the line, leave the signs up until the unit is completed.

☞ Tip:

Instead of using a written test to check students' learning at the end of a unit of instruction, ask students to create their own outline line, explaining as they post their signs or objects. They can either work individually or in small groups.

Idea 16

Three A's and a C

Here is a great way to combine a cooperative group learning structure with good questioning techniques. Three A's and a C requires students to use several levels of thinking skills, including knowledge, comprehension, analysis, syntheses, and evaluation as they answer questions. To help students remember the steps, we have called it Three A's and a C, which represents these activities:

1. Ask

2. Answer

3. Analyze, and

4. Choose

Although this idea is great for gifted students, we think it can be used effectively for all classes and that it works especially well for small groups (remember to put gifted students in groups with other gifted students at least part of the time). It is a great way to review content material at the end of a unit of study and before a test. The strategy also can be used before a unit of instruction, to find out what students already know about the topic and to increase their interest. Three A's and a C not only provides students with opportunities to answer questions, students also get practice synthesizing and evaluating information from others. This strategy works well with almost any grade level and any subject area. We have provided a Three A's and a C card for you to use to teach your students the process.

Here's how Three A's and a C works.

Ask

✪ Before class, decide on some key questions you think your students should be able to answer. You should focus on "big" questions that can have several correct answers or layers of answers that can be simple or more complex (see Idea 13, Socratic Starters).

✪ Using large pages of chart paper from tablets, write one question at the top of each page. Use large enough handwriting so that all students in the group can easily read the question. Write the same number of questions as you will have groups of students. (You may want to color-code the pages by writing each question in a different color. This will help students remember their original question and allow you to easily evaluate each group's productivity.)

Answer

✪ Next, divide students into groups. Usually, groups of three or four will work best. Assign one student per group to write responses to the question, then ask the group to choose a spokesperson, who will answer orally at the end of the activity.

✪ Give each group one piece of chart paper that has one question written at the top of the page.

✪ Using a timer or stopwatch, give students 2 to 5 minutes to read the question aloud and work as a group to generate as many answers as possible to the question.

✪ After the time is up, each group should pass their chart to the next group (e.g., the group to their right).

Analyze

✪ When each group has their new chart and question, they should read the question orally, read the previous group's answers, and then add their own responses to the list.

✪ Repeat this process until the charts are back at the original groups. Be careful of time. If students have too long to answer, they will lose focus and begin to get off task.

Choose

✪ Once each group has its original question back, ask the students to reread their original question, review all of the answers from all of the groups, and then choose the three best answers. They should be able to defend their choices by explaining why they believe the three answers they picked are best.

✪ Ask the spokesperson for each group to stand. He or she should read the question, and then tell which answers they think are the best and why.

✪ If other groups disagree, allow them to explain their position.

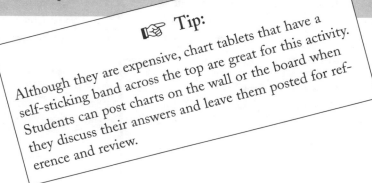

☞ Tip:
Although they are expensive, chart tablets that have a self-sticking band across the top are great for this activity. Students can post charts on the wall or the board when they discuss their answers and leave them posted for reference and review.

Three A's and a C

1. **A**sk

2. **A**nswer

3. **A**nalyze

4. **C**hoose

Three A's and a C

1. **A**sk

2. **A**nswer

3. **A**nalyze

4. **C**hoose

Idea 16

Idea 17

Create Jigsaw Groups

Much has been written on the use of cooperative groups for students. Gifted students also can profit from these groups, particularly if the students are placed in groups with other gifted students and the material is differentiated for their ability level. The jigsaw is a specific method incorporating the use of cooperative groups. Dr. Elliot Aronson, professor emeritus at the University of California in Santa Cruz, developed the technique.

Jigsaw groups work very well when students are studying a thematic unit, such as Conservation and Its Effect on the Global Community. At some point in their investigation of this thematic unit, students would certainly study the conservation of species, which can be divided in several ways, such as by region or by animal and plant type. The jigsaw technique described below is one instructional strategy that lends itself well to the study of this and similar topics and forces all students to become responsible for their own learning.

Here's how it works.

❶ Divide the class into small groups of four or five students, depending on the number of topics to be studied.

❷ Each member of each group will be given one topic in which to become an expert. With five groups, there will be five individuals, one from each group, studying the same topic. Use the Jigsaw Topics form to assign topics by number.

❸ Allow time for students to study the materials they need to understand their topic. This works best when you have study materials prepared ahead of time. For example, you might have suggested Web sites for the students to visit or magazine articles to read.

❹ After an adequate amount of time, all students studying the same topic get together and discuss what they have learned. Your role is to make sure that groups are functioning well together and that nobody is dominating the discussion or being disruptive. With time, you will want the group members to become more responsible for handling these situations.

⑤ Have all group members reconvene in their original groups. Each expert presents what he or she has learned to the rest of the group members. Group members are encouraged to ask questions to clarify important points.

⑥ Evaluate students' learning through their development of a product (see the product possibilities in Idea 3, Get Different) or by administering a short quiz.

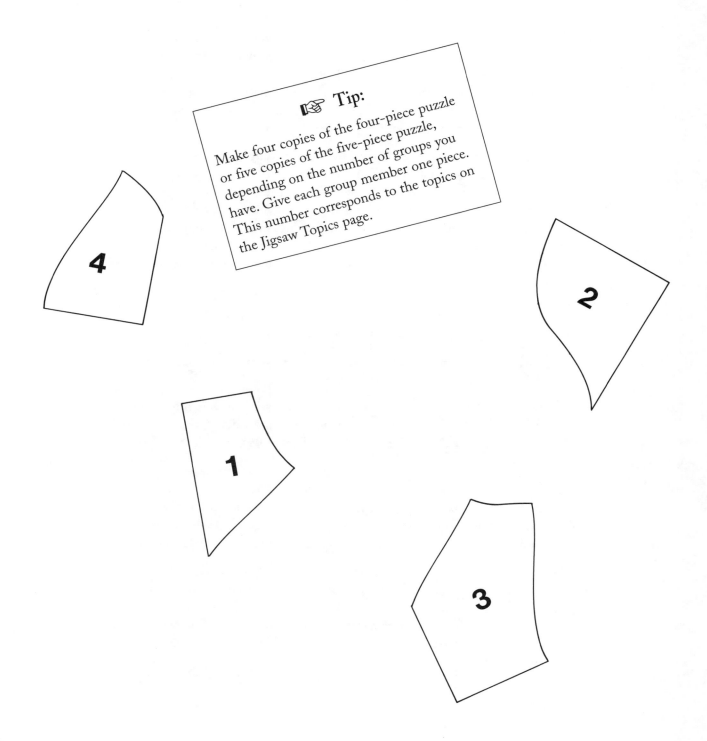

☞ Tip:

Make four copies of the four-piece puzzle, or five copies of the five-piece puzzle, depending on the number of groups you have. Give each group member one piece. This number corresponds to the topics on the Jigsaw Topics page.

4

2

1

3

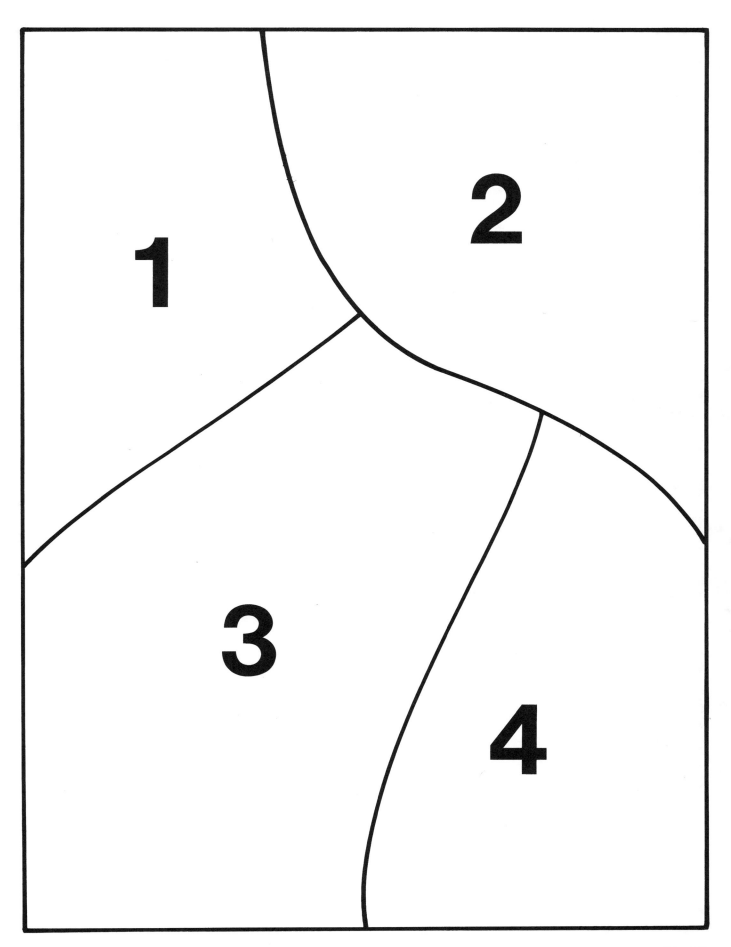

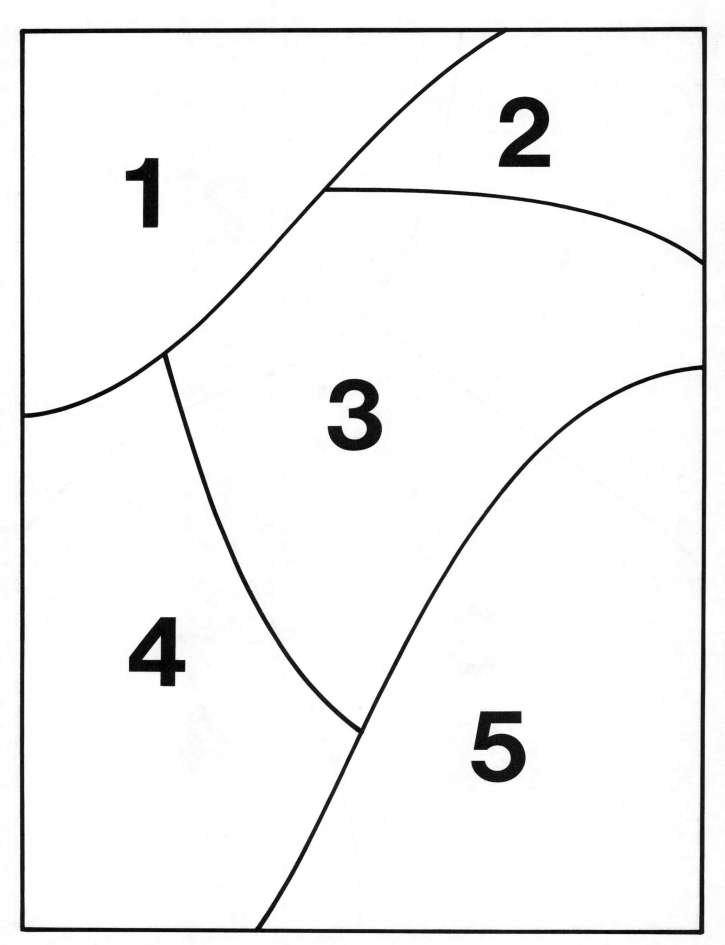

Idea 17

Jigsaw Topics

1.

2.

3.

4.

Jigsaw Topics

1.

2.

3.

4.

5.

Idea 17

Idea 18

Backwards Brainstorming

Brainstorming is a great way to generate solutions to problems. This idea, Backwards Brainstorming, varies traditional brainstorming by asking students to

- look at current solutions to problems,

- decide why they are not working, and then

- suggest new solutions that improve on the old ones.

The guide on page 111 can help you and your students stay on track throughout the process.

Here's how Backwards Brainstorming works.

❶ First, assign students to small groups. (Four students to a group works well.) Each group should appoint a recorder.

❷ Give each group a piece of chart paper with the problem you are investigating written at the top of the page. The problem can be written as a question if you wish. Also provide each group with a marker.

❸ Attach each group's chart paper to a wall, table, or easel.

❹ After reviewing the problem, ask students to state current solutions to the problem. The recorder will write the solutions on the chart paper. (You may need to prompt students with some discussion or model some ideas. For example, if you are addressing the problem of combating terrorism, talk about societal efforts that are already underway. These might include establishment of the Department of Homeland Security, mediation, and so on.)

❺ Stop after 10 minutes and ask each group to read and review all of its ideas.

❻ Next, give students 10 minutes to talk about the why each solution is not solving the problem. This should involve a quick discussion of the advantages of each idea and also its limitations. Students can use a different color marker to make brief notes about each idea on the chart paper, or you can have students use the Attribute Listing chart or T chart found in Idea 4, Critical and Creative Thinking Skills.

❼ If necessary, review the critical elements for brainstorming:
- Don't criticize
- Try to think of wild or different ideas
- Generate as many ideas as possible (quantity is important here)
- Feel free to combine your idea with someone else's to make another idea

❽ Finally, students should begin the last step of the process: Creating a new list of solutions to the problem. In a 10- to 15-minute time period, students can brainstorm a new list of solutions. Their new list should include the following:
- Improvements or modifications to current solutions
- Alternative ideas to replace current solutions that are not working at all
- Totally new and innovative solutions

Backwards Brainstorming

🐾 Follow These Steps

1. List the members of your group.

    _____
    _____
    _____
    _____

2. Write down the problem.

3. List the current solutions.

4. Read and review.

5. Identify the pros and cons of each solution.

6. Write your new ideas. Include improvements, alternatives, and new solutions.

Idea 18

Idea 19

Develop a Rubric

Probably the most common form of evaluating student learning is through criterion-referenced tests. (Don't forget that all courses or units should begin with some sort of preassessment.) Gifted students often breeze through criterion-referenced tests, answering most or all questions correctly. One reason is because these tests do not have enough ceiling to allow gifted students to show the depth of their knowledge. The next three ideas provide alternative assessment strategies so gifted students have more opportunity to show the depth and breadth of their knowledge and have more choice in how they want to be assessed.

Rubrics can be holistic or analytical. A holistic rubric is one that rates a product globally. For example, suppose you want your students to write a passage in response to a prompt. You decide to rate them holistically using a 0–5 scale. A score of 0 might be defined as *No attempt to respond to the prompt*. A score of 5 might be defined as *Writing is clear and concise*.

An analytical rubric is scored on more than one dimension and yields more diagnostic information. It is usually more useful for planning and improving instruction. This idea assists you in developing analytical rubrics.

To develop a rubric, follow these steps.

❶ **Generate the important dimensions.**
   Use our Dimension Starters as a beginning point, or examine examples of student work to help you determine the important dimensions.

❷ **Write a definition for each dimension.**
   For example, suppose you are developing a rubric for conducting a science experiment. One dimension would probably be *Conclusion*. This may be defined to include the degree to which the student effectively uses the results of the experiment to draw a sound conclusion and how well the conclusion is related to the review of the literature.

☞ **Tip:**

Ask students to create the rubric before completing a project or activity. This forces them to think about the characteristics that would demonstrate mastery.

❸ Decide on the number of levels for each dimension.
Three to five levels is usually enough to show depth, but not too many to be overwhelming. Suggestions for levels include the following: emerging, expanding, proficient, superior; unsatisfactory, acceptable, commendable, exemplary; and novice, apprentice, practitioner, expert.

❹ Identify benchmarks for each level of each dimension.
These come directly from your definition. The better you define what each dimension means, the easier it is to write good benchmarks.

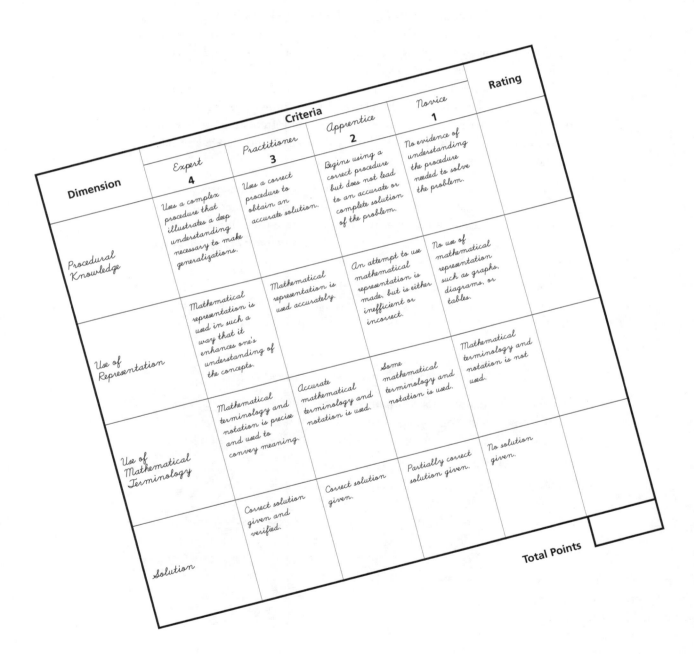

Dimension	Criteria				Rating
	Expert 4	Practitioner 3	Apprentice 2	Novice 1	
Procedural Knowledge	Uses a complex procedure that illustrates a deep understanding necessary to make generalizations.	Uses a correct procedure to obtain an accurate solution.	Begins using a correct procedure but does not lead to an accurate or complete solution of the problem.	No evidence of understanding the procedure needed to solve the problem.	
Use of Representation	Mathematical representation is used in such a way that it enhances one's understanding of the concepts.	Mathematical representation is used accurately.	An attempt to use mathematical representation is made, but is either inefficient or incorrect.	No use of mathematical representation such as graphs, diagrams, or tables.	
Use of Mathematical Terminology	Mathematical terminology and notation is precise and used to convey meaning.	Accurate mathematical terminology and notation is used.	Some mathematical terminology and notation is used.	Mathematical terminology and notation is not used.	
Solution	Correct solution given and verified.	Correct solution given.	Partially correct solution given.	No solution given.	
				Total Points	

Dimension Starters

By Subject Area

Subject Area	Dimension
Reading	Construct Meaning from Text Connections with Text Generalizes Beyond Text Summarize Use of Reading Strategies
Writing	Organization Mechanics Writes for a Purpose Use of Language
Mathematics	Conceptual Understanding Procedural Knowledge Use of Mathematical Terminology Use of Representation Solution
Science	Statement of Hypothesis Procedure Quality of Data or Observations Interpretation of Results Conclusion
Social Studies	Knowledge and Use of History Argumentation Quality of Sources Synthesis of Information Communication of Ideas

By Product

Product	Dimension
Oral Presentation	Organization Graphics Elocution Subject Knowledge
Pamphlet	Design Mechanics Quality of Information Included
Annotated Bibliography	Format Style Quality of Annotations
Photo Essay	Layout Technical Quality of Photos Relevance of Photos to Topic
Model (or other creative products)	Aesthetics Adherence to Conventions Novelty
Web Page	Consistency of Navigation Technical Quality Relevance of Information Included
Poster	Appearance Organization Ability To Convey Intention

Idea 19

Dimension	Criteria				Rating
	4	3	2	1	

Total Points

Idea 19

Dimension	Criteria			Rating
	3	2	1	

Total Points

Idea 19

Idea 20

Create a Choice Sheet

This strategy allows students choices for how they want to be assessed.

Here's how it works.

❶ Develop three levels of assessment tasks ranging from relatively easy to moderate to difficult and label these 2, 5, and 8 (or other numbers if you wish). Magner (2000) suggests that the lowest level focus on knowledge and comprehension, the moderate level on application and analysis, and the difficult level on evaluation and synthesis.

❷ Provide a minimum of three assessment choices in each level. Make sure to include a variety of choices so students can be assessed in their area of interest or strength.

❸ Decide on the number of points a student must accumulate to meet the assignment requirement. Usually a teacher will require a total of 10 points so that students must choose at least one 5 or one 8. But the total can vary depending on the type of assignment. We have provided a blank form for you to write the assessment choices and a contract for the students to complete.

Note. This idea is adapted from "Reaching All Children Through Differentiated Assessment: The 2-5-8 Plan," by L. Magner, 2000, *Gifted Child Today, 23*(3), pp. 48–50. Copyright 2000 by Prufrock Press. Adapted with permission.

Choice Sheet

Level 2

A. Present an oral interpretation of your three favorite poems to the class.

B. Prepare a PowerPoint slide show with at least eight slides with a visual interpretation of the images in your favorite poem. Share your PowerPoint presentation with the class.

C. Prepare an annotated Web site list of 10 Web sites that contain poetry for young people. Include the URL and a brief description of the site.

Level 5

A. Read and prepare an annotated bibliography of five famous poetry anthologies. Include the reference, a description of the type of poetry, and one paragraph about the author.

B. Write a paper that includes a poem illustrating each genre we studied, explains each poem's characteristics, and compares and contrasts the characteristics to the genre it is illustrating.

C. Create a brochure about your favorite author. Include a brief description of the author's life, the type of poetry the author writes or has written, and a description of how the author's writing relates to you.

Level 8

A. Write and illustrate a book of 10 original poems. Include examples of at least three genres we have studied (e.g., sonnet, narrative, lyric). Submit your two favorite poems for publication.

B. Create a photo essay illustrating five of your favorite poems. Include at least five photographs for each poem. Include a written summary explaining why each photo was included. Include your photo essay as part of our school's art show.

C. Design a learning center to help younger students enjoy and understand poetry. Determine the center's objectives; develop the activities (e.g., file folder activities, WebQuests, games, reading); prepare clear directions for the center and for each activity in the center; and construct the center. Give the center to a teacher of younger students to use.

Idea 20

Choice Sheet

....
Level 2

A.

B.

C.

....
Level 5

A.

B.

C.

....
Level 8

A.

B.

C.

Idea 20

Choice Sheet

....
Level 2

A.

B.

C.

....
Level 5

A.

B.

C.

....
Level 8

A.

B.

C.

Idea 20

Name _____ Date _____

Assignment _____

I will complete the following assessment choices.

Level 2 ❑ **A** ❑ **B** ❑ **C**

Level 5 ❑ **A** ❑ **B** ❑ **C**

Level 8 ❑ **A** ❑ **B** ❑ **C**

Name _____ Date _____

Assignment _____

I will complete the following assessment choices.

Level 2 ❑ **A** ❑ **B** ❑ **C**

Level 5 ❑ **A** ❑ **B** ❑ **C**

Level 8 ❑ **A** ❑ **B** ❑ **C**

Idea 20

Idea 21

Keep a Portfolio

Portfolios are an accumulation of a student's work over time. Portfolios can be kept in a variety of ways for a variety of purposes; however, the basic guidelines for keeping good portfolios are the same no matter what their purpose.

Here are the guidelines.

❶ Students and teachers should develop criteria for selecting and assessing the portfolio before beginning the process (see Idea 19, Develop a Rubric, for assistance in developing the assessment criteria).

❷ Portfolios contain samples of the student's work, which can be the student's best work (product portfolios) or can show the student's growth over time (process portfolios).

❸ A wide variety of materials should be included: self-reflections, audiotapes, photographs, worksheets, artwork, research papers, and videos.

❹ Students should write a brief rationale for including each item, which can relate to their performance, how they view their progress, or how they view themselves as learners.

❺ Some of the products should be optional (student choice) and some should be core (required items for all students).

Place the products in a container that makes sense for the portfolio's purpose. Containers can range from file folders to three-ring binders to file boxes. Have the students make a cover page or write a cover letter that introduces the portfolio's author and explains the purpose of the portfolio. We have provided a cover page for students to design and place at the beginning of their portfolios and reflection cards for students to include with each product.

My Portfolio

_____

Idea 21

Product Card

Name _____ Date _____

I choose to include this product because _____

_____.

This product helped me learn _____

_____.

I could improve this product _____

_____.

Product Card

Name _____ Date _____

I choose to include this product because _____

_____.

This product helped me learn _____

_____.

I could improve this product _____

_____.

Idea 21

Product Card

Name _____   Date _____

I choose to include this product because _____

_____.

This product helped me learn _____

_____.

I could improve this product _____

_____.

Product Card

Name _____   Date _____

I choose to include this product because _____

_____.

This product helped me learn _____

_____.

I could improve this product _____

_____.

Idea 22

One-Minute Quiz

It's always nice to have some quick and easy ways to assess student learning after short segments of direct instruction. The next two assessment strategies should help as you evaluate gifted students' learning after lecture, demonstration, video or computer instruction, modeling, or another instructional technique.

One-Minute Quiz

Before ending your lesson, pass out the One-Minute Quiz forms. Then give students one minute to respond to the two questions:

❶ What was the most important thing you learned during this lesson?

❷ What questions do you still have about the lesson?

By reading through the forms, teachers can quickly determine which students understood the main point of the lesson and which students will require reteaching or additional support. Teachers also will find out which parts of the lesson were not understood by many or most students. This will help guide further instruction. The one-minute time limit keeps the pacing of the lesson on track.

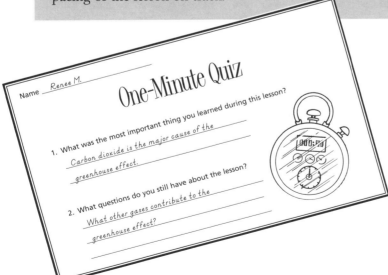

129

One-Minute Quiz

1. What was the most important thing you learned during this lesson?

   _____

   _____

2. What questions do you still have about the lesson?

   _____

   _____

   _____

Name _____

One-Minute Quiz

1. What was the most important thing you learned during this lesson?

   _____

   _____

2. What questions do you still have about the lesson?

I Don't Get It

This idea is similar to Idea 22, One-Minute Quiz. After completing a lesson or lesson segment, give students the I Don't Get It form. Ask them to fill in the blank to respond to the following question:

✪ What is one point that you did not understand in today's lesson? ✪

Again, by reading through student responses, teachers can quickly ascertain how well students understood the instruction and make plans for extending, generalizing, modifying, or reteaching the lesson.

Name: _Marshal G._

I Don't Get It

What is one point that you did not understand
in today's lesson?

How does pyruvic acid become a
two-carbon compound to enter the
Krebs cycle?

**Not everything has to be
evaluated with a test!**

Name _____

I Don't Get It

What is one point that you did not understand
in today's lesson?

_____
_____
_____
_____

Name _____

I Don't Get It

What is one point that you did not understand
in today's lesson?

_____
_____
_____
_____

Idea 24
MoD Squad
(Moral Decision Making by a Team)

There are many approaches to decision making and problem solving, some of which are provided in other ideas in this book (see Ideas 1 and 29). Whereas some of these decision-making techniques address generic problems and issues, the term "moral decision making" refers to the process of seeking solutions to dilemmas or problems while taking into account moral and ethical considerations. Learning at least one approach to moral decision making should help gifted students in two skill areas:

• Making good decisions using reasoning

• Developing strong, positive leadership skills

The MoD Squad idea is based in part on an article by Bebeau (2002) that discusses responses to moral problems in scientific research. Although Bebeau's discussion does not focus on a specific decision-making process, it is an interesting discussion of reasonable methods for solving moral problems. MoD Squad involves a six-step process. Teachers can use the MoD Squad Questions form to help guide students through the process and the MoD Squad Process form to help students present their solutions. This activity can be taught most effectively in a group format because discussion will likely yield ideas and considerations that some students might never have considered or generated individually.

Before beginning the MoD Squad process, present students with a moral dilemma. Examples of dilemmas can be found in literature related to moral reasoning (Kohlberg and others) and in Goldstein and Glick's (1987) book, *Aggression Replacement Training*. Eventually, students should suggest real-life dilemmas or problems of their own, then use the same steps to suggest solutions.

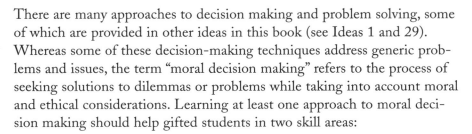

Here is a description of the six-step process.

❶ When faced with a problem or a dilemma, students should first describe the dilemma or problem. Inherent in a dilemma is the idea that the rights or obligations of interested parties conflict. To adequately analyze the dilemma, then, students should move beyond just identifying or naming the issue. Require them to analyze the facts, and then describe the nature of the moral conflict inherent in the problem. They can do this by answering questions similar to those on the MoD Squad Questions form.

❷ Next, students should identify the interested parties affected by the dilemma. Encourage students to think broadly here, so that they consider people who may not be directly involved but to whom the situation might be relevant (e.g., other individuals, the community, the country, and so on). This discussion may lead to the identification of additional facts. If so, go back to the first section of the form and add those facts to the description.

❸ Next have students generate possible solutions to the problem or actions that can be taken to alleviate the dilemma. In this part of the process, students can use brainstorming techniques or generate suggestions through group discussion.

❹ The fourth step is to explain the consequences for each solution or action. Suggest to students that they focus on those consequences that have a high probability of occurring. As they consider the consequences, students should consider each of the individuals or interested parties they identified in Step 2. Don't leave anyone out! Students also should consider both positive and negative consequences.

❺ Next, students should identify obligations that an individual would have to the various interested parties. Encourage students to go deeper than surface obligations and also to consider duty, personal responsibility, professional obligations, the nature of integrity, and so on.

❻ Finally, students should choose the best solution(s). After completing the first five steps in the process, students should be able to articulate their own or their group's solution to the dilemma or problem. In explaining their solution, it is important that they address each of the prior steps, with an emphasis on Steps 2, 4, and 5. These are the steps that give special consideration to moral reasoning and set this process apart from traditional decision-making and problem-solving models. You can use the Evaluation Form found in Idea 4, Critical and Creative Thinking Skills.

References. Bebeau, M. J. (n.d.). *Developing a well reasoned response to a moral problem in scientific research.* Retrieved June 2, 2002, from http://veghome.ucdavis.edu/classes/ggg296/moral%20reasoning.htm

Goldstein, A. P., & Glick, B., with Reiner, S., Zimmerman, D., & Coultry, T. M. (1987). *Aggression replacement training: A comprehensive intervention for aggressive youth.* Champaign, IL: Research Press.

Kohlberg, L. (1981). *Essays on moral development: The philosophy of moral development.* New York: Harper & Row.

MoD Squad Questions

Provide students with these questions as they consider a dilemma or problem.

 Describe the Dilemma or Problem
- ✔ What is the issue or conflict?
- ✔ Is there a deeper moral conflict—are there issues of right and wrong?
- ✔ Are some considerations more important than others?

 Identify the Interested Parties
- ✔ Who are the individuals directly affected by the dilemma or problem?
- ✔ How are those parties in conflict?
- ✔ Are there others who are indirectly involved but who should be considered as well?

 Generate Possible Solutions
- ✔ What actions can be taken to alleviate the situation?
- ✔ Are there some obvious solutions to the problem?
- ✔ Can you address the issue in a unique or novel way?

 Explain the Consequences of the Solutions
- ✔ What are the consequences that are most likely to happen?
- ✔ Have you identified consequences for each interested party or individual involved?
- ✔ Are there both negative and positive consequences?

 Identify Obligations
- ✔ What obligations does each interested party have to the others?
- ✔ Are there higher level obligations to principles and responsibilities beyond obligations to individuals?
- ✔ Which obligations are most important and how do you make that decision?

 Choose the Best Solution(s)
- ✔ Is there just one solution to the problem or are there several?
- ✔ Does the solution consider what is good for each of the interested parties?
- ✔ In making your decision, did you consider the obligations that individuals have to each other, to a larger group, and to other principles? If so, how much weight did you give to each?

MoD Squad Process

Step 1   **Describe the Dilemma or Problem**

_____   _____
_____   _____
_____   _____

Step 2   **Identify the Interested Parties**

_____   _____
_____   _____
_____   _____

Step 3   **Generate Possible Solutions**

_____   _____
_____   _____
_____   _____

Step 4   **Explain the Consequences of the Solutions**

_____   _____
_____   _____
_____   _____

Step 5   **Identify Obligations**

_____   _____
_____   _____
_____   _____

Step 6   **Choose the Best Solution(s)**

_____   _____
_____   _____
_____   _____

Idea 24

Idea 25

Listen To Lead

Everyone likes a good listener. And, although not all good listeners are good leaders, most great leaders have great listening skills. To help your students improve at listening, you can teach them to self-evaluate, self-monitor, and change some of their poor listening habits. We have provided a checklist for students so that they (and you) can monitor their listening skills, then target skills that need improvement.

Here are three quick and easy ideas to use with the checklist.

❶ First, videotape your class as they listen to a selected student's presentation or discussion. Later, play the videotape back and ask each student to evaluate his or her listening skills with the checklist. Help them target one or two areas for improvement.

❷ Another idea is to assign students to triads and ask them to number off: 1, 2, and 3. Student Number 1 gets 3 minutes to talk, expressing his or her view on a controversial topic (Should we use the death penalty? Is it right to allow prayer in school? and so on). As Student Number 2 listens, Student Number 3 can use the checklist to evaluate Number 2's listening skills. When 3 minutes is up, rotate the roles so that Number 2 talks, Number 3 listens, and Number 1 evaluates. Stop again after 3 minutes and rotate the roles one more time. After each student has had a turn with each role, you can guide a discussion of the whole group's strengths, weaknesses, emotional reactions to others' opinions, goals for improvement, and so on.

❸ Our last idea is very simple. Using the checklist as a teaching tool, review it with students daily or weekly. Then, at random intervals, reinforce them with the listening coupons we have provided. Coupons can be used for a weekly drawing—perhaps allowing the winners to choose music they would like to listen to.

Listen To Lead

- Look at the speaker, and use nods and comments to show that you are listening.

- Listen with your ears, your eyes, and your imagination.

- Review mentally what you already know about what the speaker is discussing.

- Try to put yourself in the speaker's place and recognize how he or she is feeling about what is being said.

- Keep an open mind by setting aside prejudices and preconceived opinions.

- Use memory techniques to help you remember what the speaker says.

- Every now and then, summarize what you have heard and check with the speaker to be sure that you have understood.

- Ask nonthreatening questions to build understanding.

Idea 25

139

Idea 25

Idea 26

Three Ways To Think About Leaders

Developing leadership skills in gifted students is often a difficult and complicated process. Teachers can begin with three related activities designed to help students:

- Identify individuals who are or were great leaders,

- Identify the qualities those leaders demonstrated, and

- Examine their own and others' beliefs about effective leadership.

To complete these activities, we have provided two tools and a related idea that should help you as you guide students' progress. The resources include a Leadership Grid, Leadership Qualities Webs, and Socratic Starters.

Activity 1: Using the Leadership Grid

The first tool, the Leadership Grid, is easy to use and can be reproduced for individual students or enlarged for a group instruction format.

❶ First, review with students the categories in which we can identify great leaders. This will help students consider traditional and common categories like politics or sports and less emphasized areas of endeavor like education or religion.

❷ Next, ask students to add an additional category in the blank space at the bottom of the first column. Encourage each student to focus on a topic or field of special interest to him or her.

❸ Third, ask students to fill in the grid by listing the names of great leaders in each category. Begin with familiar names but ask students to mention leaders who are unique or who have not necessarily received a lot of publicity or acclaim.

❹ After students have finished filling in the grid, discuss with them why they suggested the individuals whose names they included. During your discussion, address questions like:
  - Why do you think _____ is a great leader?
  - What qualities define leadership?
  - How do you think these individuals developed their leadership skills?

Activity 2: Using the Leadership Qualities Web

Once students have identified individuals they believe are great leaders, help them identify the qualities that have affected those individuals' ability to lead. Focus your discussion on qualities that enabled the leaders to

❶ Become and remain effective.

❷ Influence others.

❸ Communicate their vision for the future.

❹ Inspire others to a common purpose.

❺ Overcome problems and setbacks.

❻ Achieve their goals.

❼ Affect behaviors of a significant number of individuals.

❽ Exercise power in a group or groups.

❾ Share a high moral and ethical purpose.

To foster this discussion and support students' efforts at identifying the qualities of effective leaders, you can use the Leadership Qualities Webs. Recognize that students may identify some negative qualities of negative or destructive leaders. If so, encourage them to discuss those qualities and their long-term impact on the world or on individuals.

Activity 3: Use Socratic Starters

To complete this introductory study of leadership, use Idea 13, Socratic Starters, to guide a group discussion related to leaders and the qualities that made (make) them effective. Give special emphasis to Socratic questioning that

❶ Probes assumptions.

❷ Examines viewpoints or perspectives.

❸ Probes implications and consequences.

These questions should help students clarify their beliefs and spark further interest in leadership activities.

Leadership Grid

Field or Area of Expertise	Leaders from the Past	Today's Leaders
Education		
Science/Technology/Mathematics		
Medicine		
Politics/Government		
Humanities/Social Service		
Religion		
Sports		
Fine Arts/Design/Architecture		
Performance Arts and Entertainment		

Idea 26

Leadership Grid

Field or Area of Expertise	Leaders from the Past	Today's Leaders

Idea 26

Leadership Qualities Web

Leader _____

Area of Leadership _____

What qualities of this leader helped him or her:

Become or remain effective?

Influence others?

Leadership Qualities Web

Leader _____

Area of Leadership _____

What qualities of this leader helped him or her:

```
┌──────────────┐          ┌──────────────┐
│              │          │              │
│              │          │              │
└──────────────┘          └──────────────┘
       \                      /
        \                    /
      ┌─────────────────────────┐
      │  Communicate his or her  │
      │   vision for the future? │
      └─────────────────────────┘
        /                    \
       /                      \
┌──────────────┐          ┌──────────────┐
│              │          │              │
│              │          │              │
└──────────────┘          └──────────────┘
```

```
┌──────────────┐          ┌──────────────┐
│              │          │              │
│              │          │              │
└──────────────┘          └──────────────┘
       \                      /
        \                    /
      ┌─────────────────────────┐
      │   Inspire others to a    │
      │     common purpose?      │
      └─────────────────────────┘
        /                    \
       /                      \
┌──────────────┐          ┌──────────────┐
│              │          │              │
│              │          │              │
└──────────────┘          └──────────────┘
```

Leadership Qualities Web

Leader _____

Area of Leadership _____

What qualities of this leader helped him or her:

Overcome problems and setbacks?

Achieve his or her goals?

Idea 26

147

Leadership Qualities Web

Leader _____

Area of Leadership _____

What qualities of this leader helped him or her:

Affect the behaviors of a significant number of individuals?

Exercise power in a group or groups?

Idea 26

Leadership Qualities Web

Leader _____

Area of Leadership _____

What qualities of this leader helped him or her:

Idea 27

Promote Service Learning

It is important for all students to share their time and talent with others, and gifted students have many talents to share. Service learning combines meaningful community service with classroom learning.

Service learning has the following benefits:

- Strengthens the connection between academic learning and service

- Encourages students to make a meaningful contribution to the community

- Provides students with opportunities to learn new skills and to think critically

- Involves students in both the planning and implementation of the experience

Here are some examples of service learning.

❶ High school foreign language students tutor and create vocabulary books for elementary English as a Second Language students. Through this work, the high school students increase their knowledge of the foreign language they are studying and develop an understanding of other cultures.

❷ Middle school students in social studies class conduct research on the history of their community and interview townspeople. For their finished product they create a video for the chamber of commerce. In addition to enhancing their research skills, the students gain an understanding of their community history.

❸ Fourth graders enhance their reading and writing skills by developing ABC books with specially designed book covers for new preschoolers to their school. As part of the project, students each host a preschooler during the first week of school by being a buddy to the preschooler and spending time reading his or her ABC book together. Through this project the fourth graders meet many grade-level objectives in reading, creative writing, and critical thinking.

❹ As part of their environmental science curriculum, middle school students cultivate a community garden. They analyze the soil and learn about natural pesticides. They donate the food from the garden to the local food pantry.

One of the most important components of service learning is reflection, or the process in which students think critically about their experiences. Reflection helps students make the connection between the classroom and the community. Keeping journals is a common method used for student reflection. We have provided two journal cover pages and several suggestions to assist your students in keeping better journals. Students might enjoy illustrating the cover pages.

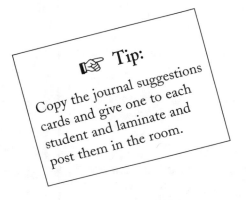

☞ Tip:

Copy the journal suggestions cards and give one to each student and laminate and post them in the room.

Note. This idea is adapted from *Project Ride: Responding to Individual Differences in Education, Elementary School Edition,* by R. Beck, 1996, Longmont, CO: Sopris West. Copyright 1996 by Sopris West. Adapted with permission.

Ingredients of a Great Journal

Journals are not:

◎ work logs of tasks, times, and dates

Journals are:

◎ snapshots of concerns, insights, and critical questions about the people involved including yourself

◎ honest reflections

◎ freely written; don't worry about grammar and spelling until the final draft

◎ something to write in after each visit

Types of Reflection

Use the questions below to help you think about what to write in your journal.

Reflect on self

☆ What have I learned about myself from this experience?

☆ How has this experience challenged stereotypes or prejudices I had?

☆ How will this experience change the way I act or think in the future?

☆ How have I been challenged?

☆ How have my ideals and philosophies changed?

Reflect on details

✤ What happened during this experience?

✤ What would I change about this situation if I were in charge?

✤ How did my actions have an impact?

✤ What more do I need to do?

✤ How does this experience help me understand what I'm learning in class?

Reflection on relationship to the world

✿ What were the overarching issues that influenced the situation?

✿ What could I do to change the situation?

✿ How will I alter my future behaviors?

✿ How is what I am involved in affected by the larger political or social sphere?

✿ What does the future hold for this issue?

Idea 27

My Journal

By

_____

Idea 27

My Journal

By

_____

157

Idea 27

Idea 27

Idea 28

Pair Students with a Mentor

Students who are gifted will often tax teachers' energy because of the pace at which they complete work and the curiosity with which they approach learning. One strategy a teacher can use is to pair a gifted student with a mentor. A mentorship is a relationship between an adult or older person and a protégé for the purposes of providing guidance and support.

Mentorships can serve a variety of purposes.

❶ They allow students to explore areas in depth with an adult or more experienced person who shares the same interest.

❷ They serve to set up internships so students can explore career interests outside of school.

❸ They support students' social–emotional development.

❹ They provide students with opportunities to access resources and facilities beyond the school walls.

These experiences can occur in school, out of school, one on one, or in small groups. They can be short—just a few weeks to provide assistance with a specific project—or they can be extended over several months to explore a career in depth. The student and the mentor can meet daily, weekly, biweekly, or even monthly.

On the next page is a checklist you can use to help choose individuals who would make good mentors, and we recommend that you have a criminal background check conducted on all potential mentors. We also have provided an application form for students to complete if they are interested in a mentorship. If the student is young (i.e., in early elementary school), the teacher or other professional might use the application form in an interview format.

Choosing a Mentor Checklist

Name of Potential Mentor _____

Location _____

Area(s) in which the person can provide a mentorship _____

_____

	Yes	No
1. Is the person willing to devote the time needed to be an effective mentor?	❑	❑
2. Does the person have the necessary knowledge and expertise needed to provide a mentorship in the area(s) noted above?	❑	❑
3. Does the person get along well with young people?	❑	❑
4. Can the person provide the constructive feedback needed to nurture the student's growth?	❑	❑
5. Will there be adequate supervision, particularly in settings with a risk factor (e.g., machine shop), for the student?	❑	❑
6. Does the person have good communication skills?	❑	❑
7. Is the person flexible?	❑	❑

Idea 28

Application for Participating in the Mentor Program

Name _____ Date _____

School _____ Grade _____

Home Address _____
Street   City   State   Zip

Telephone Number _____ E-mail _____

⚙ Area of interest _____

⚙ Why do you want to participate in a mentorship? _____
_____
_____

⚙ What classes or advanced studies have you undertaken that will assist you in this mentorship? _____
_____
_____

⚙ How did you become interested in this area? _____
_____
_____

⚙ List any work or volunteer experiences and dates (continue on back if you need additional space). _____
_____
_____
_____

⚙ List any extracurricular activities in which you participate. _____
_____
_____

⚙ Why do you think having a mentor will benefit you? _____
_____
_____

Idea 29

SMART Goals/FINE Decisions

Many gifted students are perfectionists. Although we often view perfectionism as a problem, Silverman (1983) states that the root of excellence is perfectionism. On the other hand, too much perfectionism can result in underachievement. This idea provides strategies for helping students harness their perfectionism so that it works for them rather than controlling them.

Perfectionists need assistance in establishing priorities, focusing on a selected number of activities, and setting long-term goals. One strategy to teach gifted students to write good goals is called SMART. You can post this and go over it with your students when teaching goal setting. Give the half pages we have provided to your students to remind them how to set SMART goals.

Students also may become perfectionists because they fear of failure. Therefore, we have provided a decision-making model that will assist students in examining options and making FINE decisions. (See Idea 4, Critical and Creative Thinking Skills, for an evaluation grid students can use to help them with Step 4, "E," of the FINE model.)

Reference. Silverman, L. K. (1983). Personality development: The pursuit of excellence. *Journal for the Education of the Gifted,* 6(1), 5–19.

Note. The SMART mnemonic is used with permission from the Department of Education, Tasmania. (2002). *Curriculum adaptations to provide appropriately for students who are gifted.* Retrieved June 24, 2002, from http://www.education.tas.gov.au

SMART

Check to make sure you are making SMART goals.

Specific
Is my goal short and clear? ☐

Measurable
Can I measure when I have reached my goal? ☐

Attainable
Can I break my goal down into small, achievable steps? ☐

Relevant
Is my goal important to me? ☐

Time-framed
Can I set a beginning date and an expected attainment date? ☐

Idea 29

SMART

Check to make sure you are making SMART goals.

Specific
Is my goal short and clear? ☐

Measurable
Can I measure when I have reached my goal? ☐

Attainable
Can I break my goal down into small, achievable steps? ☐

Relevant
Is my goal important to me? ☐

Time-framed
Can I set a beginning date and an expected attainment date? ☐

SMART

Check to make sure you are making SMART goals.

Specific
Is my goal short and clear? ☐

Measurable
Can I measure when I have reached my goal? ☐

Attainable
Can I break my goal down into small, achievable steps? ☐

Relevant
Is my goal important to me? ☐

Time-framed
Can I set a beginning date and an expected attainment date? ☐

FINE

Check to make sure you are making FINE decisions.

Figure out the problem.
Have I figured out the exact problem that is causing trouble?

Identify solutions.
What are possible ways I can solve the problem?

Name the positives and negatives of each solution possibility.
Can I break my goal down into small, achievable steps?

Evaluate the solutions to decide which is best.
Have I identified the solution with the most positives and fewest negatives?

166

FINE

Check to make sure you are making FINE decisions.

Figure out the problem.
Have I figured out the exact problem that is causing trouble? ☐

Identify solutions.
What are possible ways I can solve the problem? ☐

Name the positives and negatives
of each solution possibility. ☐
Can I break my goal down into small, achievable steps?

Evaluate the solutions to decide which is best. ☐
Have I identified the solution with the most positives
and fewest negatives?

FINE

Check to make sure you are making FINE decisions.

Figure out the problem.
Have I figured out the exact problem that is causing trouble? ☐

Identify solutions.
What are possible ways I can solve the problem? ☐

Name the positives and negatives
of each solution possibility. ☐
Can I break my goal down into small, achievable steps?

Evaluate the solutions to decide which is best. ☐
Have I identified the solution with the most positives
and fewest negatives?

Idea 29

Idea 30

What Can Parents and Teachers Do To Foster Talent?

This last idea is a list of suggestions to help parents and teachers foster talent in their children and students. We have provided these suggestions in the four areas covered by the rating scale. Copy the suggestions and give them to other teachers and students' parents to help them work more effectively with their gifted children and students.

What Can Parents Do?

General Intellectual Ability

1. Listen actively to your child's ideas and show genuine enthusiasm about his or her observations, interests, and activities.
2. Encourage your child to question.
3. Provide mutual trust and approval.
4. Provide your child with opportunities to participate in outside activities, but avoid overscheduling your child's time.
5. Visit the library.
6. Join a gifted children's advocacy group.
7. Become involved in your child's school.
8. Be a lifelong learner.
9. Stimulate your child's intellectual capabilities through exposure to books, travel, technology, and the arts.
10. Remember, no matter what your child's gifts, he or she is still a child.

Specific Academic Aptitude

1. Find out what your child's interests are and share them with his or her teachers.
2. Help your child to negotiate with his or her teacher. Teach him or her these steps: Set up an appointment and be on time. State your feelings politely and provide specific examples. Be willing to compromise.
3. Allow your child to pursue interests that may not be typical of others his or her age.
4. Provide materials that encourage your child in his or her area of interest.
5. Help your child understand the relationship between effort and outcome.
6. Consider acceleration, dual enrollment, distance learning, and other similar options when your child has already mastered the content.
7. Advocate for your child.
8. Read widely in your child's area of strength.
9. Find a mentor for your child.
10. If possible, get a home computer with Internet access.

Creativity

1. Provide your child with new experiences.
2. Provide a private place for your child to pursue creative work.
3. Provide materials for your child to engage in creativity.
4. Encourage curiosity and fantasy.
5. Display your child's creative work.
6. Laugh with your child and encourage a good sense of humor.
7. Allow your child to be different.
8. Teach your child that hard work and discipline are important ingredients for creativity.
9. Play with your child and create a sense of escape and adventure.
10. Provide an environment that allows your child to explore.

Leadership

1. Encourage your child to volunteer in the community.
2. Encourage your child to participate in extracurricular activities.
3. Enroll your child in pressure-free, noncompetitive summer activities.
4. Maintain a consistent set of values.
5. Show your child how to set priorities.
6. Model goal setting and decision making.
7. Help your child examine issues from many viewpoints.
8. Talk often with your child and allow him or her to ask questions.
9. Promote friendships with individuals of all ages and cultures.
10. Respect your child's ideas.

Idea 30

What Can Teachers Do?

General Intellectual Ability

1. Listen actively to your students and show genuine enthusiasm about their observations, interests, and activities.
2. Teach students how to think by focusing on significant content.
3. Practice flexibility.
4. Stay current and seek additional training in gifted education.
5. Ask open-ended questions.
6. Use problem-based learning.
7. Focus on the process rather than product.
8. Make learning an active process.
9. Emphasize the big ideas.
10. Welcome parents to assist in your classroom.

Specific Academic Aptitude

1. Pretest at the beginning of a new unit of study.
2. Compact the curriculum.
3. Consider acceleration as an option.
4. Use instructional strategies such as discovery, problem solving, and discussion; use little or no drill and practice.
5. Use flexible grouping practices; do not rely solely on heterogeneous grouping.
6. Use learning contracts.
7. Show enthusiasm and stay current in your subject area.
8. Find mentors for students in their area of expertise or interest.
9. Teach students how to critically evaluate their own work.
10. Use authentic assessment.

Creativity

1. Start class with a creative warm-up activity.
2. Use rewards sparingly.
3. Provide ample reflection time.
4. Create a learning environment where students are encouraged to dream and use their imagination.
5. Teach creative problem solving through the use of problems that occur in everyday life.
6. Encourage risk taking (as long as it will not put the student in danger).
7. Respect students' unusual questions, ideas, and solutions.
8. Promote the concept that mistakes are learning opportunities.
9. Model tolerance of ambiguity.
10. Allow students time to play with ideas.

Leadership

1. Create an environment where students feel comfortable talking about their concerns.
2. Teach decision-making skills.
3. Assist in setting goals.
4. Model high moral and ethical behavior.
5. Require community involvement (service learning).
6. Teach communication skills (both speaking and listening).
7. Study eminent leaders.
8. Model a healthy compliance to truth and fairness.
9. Help students find self-acceptance and recognize their strengths and weaknesses.
10. Provide career guidance.

Idea 30